# The Excellency of a Gracious Spirit

## A Treatise on Numbers 14:24

"A man of understanding is
of an excellent spirit."
Proverbs 17:27

by JEREMIAH BURROUGHS
*Minister of God's Word*

Edited by Dr. Don Kistler

SOLI DEO GLORIA PUBLICATIONS
*. . . for instruction in righteousness . . .*

Soli Deo Gloria Publications
A division of Ligonier Ministries
P.O. Box 547500, Orlando, FL 32854
(407) 333-4244/ FAX 333-4233
www.ligonier.org

ISBN 1-57358-024-4

Library of Congress Cataloging-in-Publication Data

Burroughs, Jeremiah, 1599-1646.
  The excellency of a gracious spirit : a treatise on Numbers
14:24 / by Jeremiah Burroughs ; edited by Don Kistler.
      p. cm.
  Previously published: Morgan, PA : Soli Deo Gloria Publications,
c1995.
  Includes bibliographical references.
  ISBN 1-57358-024-4 (alk. paper)
  1.  Christian life–Congregational authors. 2.  Bible. O.T.
Numbers XIV, 24–Criticism, interpretation, etc.
I. Kistler, Don. II. Title.

BV4501.3.B875 2006
248.4'859–dc2
                     2006012807

# Contents

## Part I: What That Other Spirit Is

# The Epistle Dedicatory

Right Honorable,

There is a common slander that has been raised, and vile aspersion that has been, and still is, cast upon the ways of godliness: that they disenable men's spirits (which Salvian complained of eleven hundred years ago: "If anyone from the nobility began to turn to God, he immediately sends away the honor of the nobility. Oh, how great is the honor of Christ in Christian people when religion makes them ignoble!), that they make men rigid, melancholy, sour, and uncivil; that they dull their parts; that they take them off from the delights of the things in the world; that if men take up the power and strictness of them they must resolve to never keep any correspondence with their friends who are of rank and quality in the world. And therefore, although those who have little of the world, and little to do in the world, may live strict lives, yet it is not for such who are born to great things, whose fortunes are raised higher than other men's, who have references to many of quality and place. It cannot be expected that they should be so strict. This must hinder them in their outward accomplishments. If they begin to take such a course, it is impossible they should be complete in every way, as becomes such as they are. And thus many are compelled to be evil lest they should be esteemed vile, as Salvian complains of his time, "Evil men think they have to be worthless." This was a notable speech of his, fully suitable to our times. The first observance that I remember I had of this place in Salvian was from your Lordship's own hands, showing it to me in him as an expression that your Lordship was much affected with. But these men do not consider how much they speak against themselves. Were this true, it would be a snare, a judgment to be raised in outward excellencies above others. No, it is not honor; they are not riches, parts, or dignities that hinder godliness. It is the baseness and corruption of men's spirits in their enjoyment of these that hinders. Godliness raises the excellencies of them. It draws out the chief good in them and puts a higher beauty and glory upon them. God has raised up Your Honor to convince the world of the falseness, malice, and impiety that there is in this evil report that is brought upon the good and blessed ways of godliness.

Malice itself cannot but acknowledge that godliness, in the strictness of it and natural excellence, in the eminence of it, has a blessed conjunction in Your Honor. Godliness is as the enameling of pearls in those golden, natural endowments with which God has mercifully and plentifully enriched you. And were it but for this service only to God and His church in convincing the world of the vileness of this slander (I may speak without suspicion of flattery), happy that ever you were born. And I do know that those who know Your Lordship will justify me in what I say. In this God has honored Your Lordship exceedingly. Were there no other end for which you still live in such a generation as you do but this, yet in this you have great cause to bless yourself in God, and in this great honor He has put upon you: to make you so public and worthy an instrument of His.

Who is it that looks upon you and sees your ways but must confess, "Now I see that strictness and power of religion may stand with a most generous, sweet, amiable, and courteous demeanor. I see it raises and ennobles parts and, though it banishes base and sordid pleasures, which are beneath the dignity of man, much more of true nobility and generosity, yet it knows how to make use of the delights that God affords in this world, and orders and guides them so that by it they are enjoined with a double sweetness far above that which others find."

And yet, further, there are two more blessed conjunctures that add much honor to you. The one is a facile yieldableness of spirit to any (though much inferior) in anything where good may be done, and yet a strong, unmovable, steadfast, resolute spirit against that which is evil. It was the high commendation that Nazianzen gave of Athanasius, that he was, a loadstone in his sweet, gentle, drawing nature, and yet an adamant in his resolute, stout carriage against those who were evil.

The other is this, which makes all beautiful and lovely indeed: though God has raised you high in birth, in abilities, and in the esteem of men both good and bad, yet the luster of the humility of your spirit shines beautifully through all, manifesting itself in much gentleness and meekness; and this is the height of all true excellency.

"A man of understanding is of an excellent spirit," said Solomon in Proverbs 17:27. The word in the original is "a cool spirit." The Lord carry on your truly noble and generous spirit, that you may long hold forth the power, beauty, and excellency of His grace. Let the height of all your designs be to lift up the name of the great God. 2 Corinthians 5:9: "We labor," said the apostle, "whether present or absent, to be accepted of Him." The word translated "labor" loses the elegance of it. It is: "we love the honor of it." It is such a labor as we account it our honor and glory. We are ambitious. To have high designs for God is a holy and blessed ambition, whereas the ambition of other men is low and base. Account yourself blessed when God is blessed. It was the blessing of Shem in Genesis 9:26: "Blessed be the Lord God of Shem." The chief of Shem's blessings was that his Lord God was blessed.

That which I seek is to engage Your Lordship for God, and to stir you up to answer fully the esteem of expectations that men have of you, whose eyes are upon you as a public blessing, and an ornament to the profession of the truth.

And yet this I desire Your Lordship to consider, as I know you do, that religion is a greater honor and ornament to you than you are to it. It does and will honor you more than ever you did or can honor it. Your birth made you honorable, but, oh, how honorable have you been since you have been precious in God's eyes (Isaiah 43:4). Your parts were always hopeful, but how apparently have they been raised since grace has sanctified them!

Although God takes it well at the hands of those whom He has raised in the things of the world higher than others, when He sees them forward in setting out His praise, yet He would not have them think that He is beholden to them, as if the honor of God depended so upon them as it would fail did they not put to their help. No, God can raise His honor by other means. He can glorify Himself and get Himself a great name by low, mean, and contemptible things. It is not because God has need of honor from you, but because He delights to honor you that He is pleased to use you in His service. It is an advancement to whatever greatness you have in the world to be employed for God, were it but in the meanest service He has to do. Where the heart is right, even in that it glories more than in all the dignity that earth can put upon it. But yet the greater instruments the Lord raises up for His glory, the greater service He calls them unto, the greater things may we hope He intends for His church.

When Saint John saw the elders casting down their crowns before the throne saying, "Thou art worthy, O Lord, to receive glory, and honor and power" (Revelation 4:11), soon afterwards John heard every creature in heaven and on earth and sea saying, "Blessing, honor, glory, and power be unto Him that sitteth upon the throne, and unto the Lamb forever more" (Revelation 5:13). And soon after that, he saw Christ with His crown upon Him going forth conquering and to conquer (Revelation 6:2).

What great mercies might we expect, did we see God raising up truly noble and generous spirits more generally in the great ones of the earth? Did we see the elders and nobles casting down their crowns before the throne of the Lamb, willing to deny all their glory, and excellencies, and estates for the raising up of the glory of Jesus Christ?

Certainly God has greater things to do in this latter age of the world, and He is a God with whom there is as great an abundance of Spirit as ever. When His time comes, how soon will such a thing be as the raising of men's spirits to higher and more noble designs than we can now imagine?

Observing the frame and work of your most precious noble spirit, Right Honorable, put me upon the thoughts of this argument. The chief book that I made use of for the enlarging of my meditations (next to the Scripture) was that which I joyfully beheld in yourself and your noble and much honored Lady, highly honored and loved, and that deservedly, in the esteem and hearts of all who know her and the Truth (2 John 1).

Such gracious principles appeared in your spirits, such divine rules by which you were guided, those high and noble employments in which you delighted, those blessed qualifications which as so many diamonds in their luster and beauty sparkled that light, that freeness, that strength, that publicness, that holiness. Those comforts of a higher nature than the common drossy comforts of the world that you chose for yourselves, to satisfy your spirits in, and found contentment in the enjoyment of; that caused the dilating of my thoughts about these things, and now making known themselves publicly, they crave patronage from Your Lordship, who has been the original from whence they came.

And here I humbly present them to Your Honor, and to your virtuous and noble Lady, as a glass wherein you and others may see the frame and workings of your spirits. I dare say that all who know you, and know that I had the happiness to be so near unto you and to have such interest in you, will say that I had my chief help in this argument from yourselves, so that if any shall be at all affected in reading these few notes of mine, I may say to him as was said once to one who was delighted in hearing an artificial imitation of the sweet note of the nightingale, "What if you heard the nightingale herself?" So I say, what if you saw the workings of the gracious, sweet amiableness, true nobleness, generosity of such spirits themselves? Such a sight I bless God I have seen, and I shall endeavor to stir up others to bless God with me for it. And now that I might have occasion to make an honorable and thankful mention of your names, I have presumed to make my private thoughts public to the world, and to present them to Your Lordship, humbly craving pardon for this bold attempt, and so resting,

June 30, 1638
Your Honor's in all humble
and due observance,
*Jeremiah Burroughs*

# To the Christian Reader

*T*he church on earth is ever militant, continually assaulted by the dragon and his angels. Their power and policy are only improved against it. The Scripture tells us of "principalities, powers, rulers of darkness, spiritual wickedness in high places" (Ephesians 6), which are the officers of the god of this world appointed to do mischief. It tells us of the methods, devices, wiles, and depths of Satan; of errors, strong delusions, damnable heresies, and doctrines of devils which are to deceive. Through Satan and his instruments, many are wounded; many are deceived in this age, as in former ages. Does not the foundation of the Church and kingdom of Christ shake? Is not the hour of temptation upon the world? It behooves us to look unto our spirits. If they are not choice and gracious, we shall faint in the evil day.

This book reveals what a choice and gracious spirit is, that so knowing yourself you may receive encouragement, if right, or be incited to look about you, if false.

Are you endued with such a spirit as here you may find? Nothing in the world, in hell, or in your flesh shall be able to conquer you. Like Christ Himself, you shall endure such crosses and contradiction of sinners as these times are big with. You shall despise the shame and be able to resist to blood, if God shall call you to that honor.

What excellency of spirit was in Paul when he took it ill that they dissuaded him from going up to Jerusalem, where he was to meet with sharp afflictions? "What mean you to weep and break my heart?" said he, "for I am ready not to be bound only, but also to die at Jerusalem for the name of the Lord Jesus Christ" (Acts 21:13). Moses refused to be called the son of Pharaoh's daughter, though he himself or some of his posterity might happily have come to the kingdom by it, and chose afflictions rather with the people of God. He would not become an Egyptian, though of the royal stem, but remained a Hebrew, who were abominations to the Egyptians. "He knew that the reproach of the members did redound to the head, and would be well recompensed by him, and therefore he would suffer afflictions and esteemed the reproaches of Christ above all the treasures of Egypt a greater patrimony," said Ambrose. So base are many spirits in this age that they would rather censure than trace his practice.

Scaliger tells of a tree to which, when a man comes, the branches close tightly, but when he departs, the branches open up again (*Exercit.* 181. 27, 28). Too many Christians are like this tree. When any ministers or Christians who have the reproach of Christ upon them come near them and have to deal with them, let relations, promises, or engagements be what they will, they shrink themselves up and are troubled, saddened, and perplexed, thinking it a disgrace to them to have to do with such. But when they are gone, then their hearts dilate again and their faces grow pleasant. Such an adulterous generation there is that are ashamed of Christ in many of His poor, reproached, and despised members; and not only ashamed, but like that plant called the "Tartarean Lamb," which in shape and proportion answers the lamb, but grazes and eats up the grass round about it, suffering no green thing to be near. And these men are lambs in shape, but eating up every green thing that is near unto them. Psalm 14:4: "They eat up my people as bread. They are the food their malice feeds upon."

It is observed that the Pope was so busy and hot against Luther that he neglected to look to all Christendom against the Turks. Such baseness was in this Pope's breast that he could more easily have digested Mohammedism than Lutheranism; and may we not think that the Koran would be welcome to those confessors who have enjoined their burden in conscience to burn their Bibles for penance? This some who are living know to be a truth. There is much baseness in the spirits of men, and upon little occasion it vents itself. Doeg had a malicious, murderous spirit in him, and spared not those who wore the linen ephod. The rich man, Luke 12:19, was all for earth and nothing for heaven. A great man, finding his sickness increasing, caused his bed to be made between or upon his coffers, where he had much gold. A lord came to him and wished him to go to his chamber and not lie there. His answer was, "I am well where I am, so long as I can tarry, for I am near to my friends," meaning his coffers and his gold. What drossy, corporal souls such men have!

The Gadarenes drove Christ out of their country. They esteemed their swine above a Savior. Demas embraced the present world. Ananias and Sapphira reserved a portion for themselves. Such spirits ever have been, and will be, in the world. These spirits are as much beneath common reason as those mentioned in this work are above it. It is choice, not common, spirits that will honor God in stormy times.

Had not a choice and excellent spirit been in Nehemiah, the plots and practices of the enemies would have daunted him, but take a view of his spirit: "Should such a man as I am flee? And who is there, that being as I am, would go into the Temple to save his life? I will not go in" (Nehemiah 6:11). He had a good cause, a good conscience, and a good God, which advanced his spirit to such resolve that he would not take sanctuary and disparage either of them by his fear or faint-heartedness. When he saw the Sabbath profaned, he hid not his eyes from it, but contended with the nobles about it.

What divine spirits were in the three children (Daniel 3:18)? Could Nebuchadnezzar's greatness, mandates, or threats of the fiery furnace force their spirits to false worship? "Be it known unto thee, O king, that we will not serve thy gods." Here they obediently disobeyed, knowing that nothing pleases God but what He has commanded in His Word. They would not deliberate in this case. "We are not careful to answer thee," said they.

When any enticements come to draw us from the worship of God, we should stop our ears and charm the charmers never so wisely.

Charles the Emperor, and two great persons in this kingdom, soliciting King Edward VI to allow his sister, the Lady Mary, to have mass, he would not listen but bade them be content, for he would spend his life and all that he had rather than agree and grant that which he knew certainly to be against the truth. The suit being yet pressed, he burst out into bitter weeping and sobbing, desiring them to desist. The motioners, seeing his zeal and constancy, wept as fast as he, and told one that he had more divinity in his little finger than they had in all their bodies.

What a choice spirit was in that young Lord Harrington, who was a man of prayer! He prayed twice a day in secret, twice with his servants in his chamber, and joined at appointed times with the family in prayer. He would never be idle, but always well, if not religiously employed. He meditated on four or five sermons every day, retaining five or six in his memory always. He kept an exact account of his life every day, very conscientious of honoring God to purpose in public and private. On the Lord's Day he would repeat both the sermons with his servants before supper and write them down in his night book before he slept; and on the morning of that day he would, as he made himself ready, repeat those sermons he had heard the Lord's Day before. He received the Sacrament very frequently, and always fasted the Saturday before, spending the whole day in examination, prayer, and humbling himself that he might be fitted to feast with Christ. He gave away the tenth part of his estate unto the poor and to pious uses, besides his occasional charity when he was abroad. Here was a choice spirit, beautified with a variety of graces, not unfit for great and mean to propound for their pattern.

Daniel in Babylon would not defile himself with the portion of the king's meat, nor with the wine that he drank. He would rather eat vegetables than defile his conscience. When the writing was signed, the lion's den threatened, did he muffle up his religion and shrink up his spirit? He would not shut up his window nor diminish his prayers, but thrice a day prayed and gave thanks unto his God as he did aforetime. Here was a spirit for God and His ways, and not for the times.

Some temporizing politician will perhaps charge Daniel of indiscretion. No, it was the excellency of his spirit that in case of danger, and that of life, he would not separate external profession from inward faith when God would lose by it. And what? Do you charge him with indiscretion whom the Scripture commends for his wisdom? It was a proverbial speech, "Wiser than Daniel" (Ezekiel 28:3), and his heart did not accuse him for that indiscretion when he was in the lion's den, for he said, "Innocence was found in me." He was not ashamed of his godliness that had raised him, and he would maintain the honor of it.

Such spirits have true excellency in them, and are not shy of the ways or servants of God when the floods of iniquity overflow and threaten to bear down all.

Fearfulness to appear in God's cause is a part of the old man, and when God puts into him a new spirit, that ends your fearfulness. The more you have of God's Spirit, the more your old timorous, cowardly spirit is abated. As Matthew 9:16 shows, that which is put in to fill up takes from the garment, and when grace fills up a man it takes away from the old man the old baseness, fear and dastardliness in the cause of God, and a holy, undaunted resolution is begotten in you to justify wisdom, although you damn yourself.

According to the fullness of men's spirits are their carriages, with more or less confidence in their undertakings. If Satan has filled the heart, men will boldly serve him. Acts 5:3: "Why hath Satan filled thy heart to lie unto the Holy Ghost?" Satan had filled his heart, and therefore he feared not to lie to God Himself. Dieu said upon this place that it should read: "Who is he that hath filled his heart?" In our translations it is "that durst presume in his heart to do so?" Haman's heart was filled with malice, and that made him bold to attempt the destruction of all the Jews. And where godliness fills the heart, there will be venturous and bold attempts for God. Paul, being filled with the Holy Ghost, set his eyes on Elymas (Acts 13:9–10), and so thundered and lightninged against him that immediately his proud, malicious spirit was blasted.

When the heart of a man is filled with divine truths, the presence of men in highest place cannot daunt it. Elisha had a double portion of the spirit of Elijah, and did the greatness or wickedness of Jehoram daunt him? There appeared a deity in his very speech and spirit. 2 Kings 3:14: "As the Lord of Hosts liveth, before whom I stand, surely were it not that I regard the presence of Jehoshaphat, the King of Judah, I would not look towards thee nor see thee." He had a fullness of God's Spirit in him that he could speak thus to one of the gods on earth.

When a man's heart is filled with divine influence, he fears not the enemies of goodness, neither is he ashamed of all that accompanies godliness. 2 Timothy 1:7–8: "God hath given us the Spirit of power, of love, and of a sound mind; be not thou therefore ashamed of the testimony." When the power of God is in a man's spirit, he will not be ashamed of the cross, nor refuse to share in the afflictions of the gospel.

It is the honor of religion to have such disciples as will own her and stand for her at all times, and that with an undaunted courage. Acts 4:8–11: "Peter was filled with the Holy Ghost, and said, Be it known unto you all, and all the people of Israel, that by the name of Jesus Christ of Nazareth, whom you crucified, whom God raised from the dead, even by him doth this man here stand before you whole: this is the Stone which was set at nought of you builders." And later, when he and John were commanded to be silenced, what did they say? Acts 4:19–20: "Whether it be right in the sight of God, to hearken unto you more than God, judge ye; for we cannot but speak the things we have seen and heard."

It is a brand upon Nicodemus that he came to Christ by night, and so of the chief rulers who believed on Him; but the Pharisees did not confess Him lest they should be put out of the synagogues. But it was Nicodemus' praise that he later got boldness to speak for Christ when vilified, though he himself suffered much reproach for it. This showed some excellency and growth in his spirit that he could both speak and suffer for Christ.

So Joseph of Arimathea was timorous (John 19:38), but being filled with grace, "He went in boldly to Pilate and craved the body of Jesus" (Mark 15:43). With what holy boldness did those men march through reproaches, afflictions, and persecutions for the truth's sake!

Reader, swallow this book as Ezekiel did his roll, and you shall be enabled to do as much. Fill your spirit with the precious truths contained in this little treatise, and you shall find your drooping spirit to receive a heavenly warmth to come upon you, and a holy boldness thrusting you forward for God and godliness.

Wickedness is too bold and godliness too shame-faced. It has lost and suffered much through men's cowardliness.

Read, meditate, and feast your spirit with what you herein find, and you may walk bold as a lion through the midst of a crooked and perverse generation. You shall daunt wickedness itself and make religion truly beautiful and honorable.

If you should say, "This book should have been kept in, there are too many already," I answer you, there are many, but few to purpose. The sea is full of water, yet God adds to it daily by rivers and showers. Many would read little if new books were not set forth daily. Books quicken up a drowsy age to the best purpose. New books are like new fashions, taken up at first with affection.

Notwithstanding all the ammunition of the kingdom, new ammunition is made daily. Books are more needful than arms. The one defends the body, the other the soul. If your spirit is choice and right, you will acknowledge this work to be solid, spiritual, and such as you have not met with many like it.

If trees are known by their fruit, what other sentence may be passed upon the composer of it but that he has profited in the school of Christ above thousands; he has had a large operation of God's Spirit in his own soul, attained to a choiceness and excellency of spirit himself, and that he has clearly differentiated between precious and base spirits?

I shall appeal to you, Christian reader, when you have perused this book, whether you would have it buried in the dark or not. If he deserves a curse that withholds corn (Proverbs 11:26), you will bless God for the corn this author has sent to market. God made him a fountain not to be sealed up, but to flow for common good. In a fountain sealed and treasures hid, the author knew, was little profit. He has let out himself to your advantage, taken this off from his own spirit to put upon yours.

Do endeavor to better yourself by it, and if you get any good, give glory unto God. If you receive none, suspect your spirit and spare your censures. The author's spirit is above them and counts it a very small thing to be judged of man's judgment. My prayers are that you may profit much, attain true excellency of spirit, and follow God fully all your days so that your end may be comfortable and glorious.

Your Christian Friend,

*William Greenhill*

# A Gracious Spirit Is a Choice and Precious Spirit. What That Other Spirit Is

*"But My servant Caleb, because he had another spirit with him, and hath followed me fully, him will I bring into the land, wherein he went; and his seed shall possess it."*

NUMBERS 14:24

# What that Other Spirit Is that a Godly Man Has that Makes Him Different from the World

*"But My servant Caleb, because he had another spirit with him, and hath followed Me fully, him will I bring into the land, wherein he went, and his seed shall possess it."*

NUMBERS 14:24

*I*n these words we have God's approbation of Caleb, accepting his faithful service in the testimony he gave of the good land; encouraging the hearts of his people to go into it. As for the others that were sent, God determined against them that they shall never see that good land, "But My servant Caleb. . . ."

Let us consider, first, God's commendation of Caleb, and, second, His blessing upon him.

For the first point, He says three things of him:

He is My servant.

He has another spirit.

He has followed Me fully.

3

"He is My servant." It is a great honor to be the servant of the blessed God, and to be acknowledged so by God Himself. We should not look at our services to God only as duties enjoined, but as high privileges, as dignities put upon us so that we should glory in His service. It was a part of that glorious reward of those who came out of great tribulation, who washed their robes and made them white in the blood of the Lamb, that they should be before the Lord and serve Him night and day (Revelation 7:14–15).

"My servant." He has shown himself to be My servant indeed. I will forever own him. Whatever others did, he continued faithful with Me. To be a servant unto the Lord is an honor, but to be acknowledged to be faithful is a higher honor. "I have obtained mercy to be faithful," said Saint Paul in 1 Timothy 1:13, 16. To be faithful in service is not only a means of obtaining mercy, but it is a great obtained mercy.

"My servant Caleb." Caleb only is mentioned here, and so in the former chapter, verse 30.

Why is not Joshua mentioned likewise, for surely he followed the Lord fully as well as Caleb?

Some think that Joshua at first concealed himself, although afterwards He declared Himself fully; but certainly this would have been a very great sin of his, to conceal himself in such a cause of God, to have remained neutral so as to save himself. He would not have passed without some signification of God's displeasure against him for this. But in verse 30, God promises Joshua that he shall enter into the land together with Caleb. Others, therefore, think that at first Caleb was the more forward because he was of the more honorable tribe, one of the chief of the tribe of Judah; and Joshua was of Ephraim. And besides, Joshua being Moses' minister to attend on him, it might be the more suspected that he might speak to gratify

Moses, against whom the people now murmured because of the straits they were brought into by him. And besides, others think that Moses here related this narrative by Joshua—that Joshua was used in the penning of this relation—and therefore the less is said concerning Joshua.

"Another spirit." The spirits of the rest were base and cowardly, poor, dead, unworthy spirits. But he had another spirit and went not that way. There is a strange conceit some of the Jewish interpreters have of this other spirit. They say Caleb and Joshua, when they were in the land and in their journey, said as the rest of the spies did, and concealed their purpose of declaring any other opinion they had of the land that differed from the others. This they did for fear of their lives; but when they came before Moses and the children of Israel, then they had another spirit and spoke plainly what they thought. Many such chaffy interpretations of Scripture we find among them, God having given them over to the spirit of blindness.

"He followed Me fully." The words are "He fulfilled to follow Me." Nothing could take him off from Me. Whatever, therefore, becomes of the rest, he shall possess the land, and his seed with him.

I intend only to handle the two later commendations of Caleb:

First, that he was a man of "another spirit."

Second, that "he followed God fully."

I will deal with these points first separately, and then in reference to each other.

**DOCTRINE. It is the excellency of godly men to be men of other spirits, of choice spirits, differing from the common spirits of the world.** 1 Corinthians 2:12: "We have not received the spirit of the world," says the apostle, "but the spirit which is of God." There is a great deal of difference between our spirits

and the common spirits of the world. There is a vile spirit rul-
ing in the world. Ephesians 2:2: "A spirit that works strongly
and actively in the children of disobedience." But of the godly
it may be said, as it was of Daniel, 6:3, "an excellent spirit was
found in him." So surely an excellent spirit is found in them.

In this first chapter I will show what this other spirit is. In
the following chapters I will show wherein the excellency of it
lies and then make application.

First, this other spirit has other principles, a better principle than the spirit of the world. The spirits of worldly men
have base, corrupt principles by which they judge things, by
which they are led, and according to which they favor and relish whatever is propounded to them. The vileness and power
of these appear in the ways of the world, but the spirits of the
godly are acted upon by divine, heavenly, holy principles that
carry them to God, to divine and heavenly things. They carry
them by a kind of natural instinct. The frame of their spirits is
so principled that by, as it were, a natural instinct (by natural, I
mean the new nature), they favor spiritual and heavenly things.
Their hearts work after them, close with them, unite themselves
to them, find much sweetness and contentment in them, are
fastened and settled unto them. What is the reason the same
truths propounded and set before divers spirits, whose natural
parts are equal, cause one to see much excellency, receive and
relish them, while the other looks on them as mean and foolish things, wondering what men see and find in them? They
are unsavory to them; their hearts turn away from them. This is
from their divers principles.

Where the spirit is well principled, it is carried on sweetly
and strongly in God's ways. Though the natural parts are weak,
though objections against them are many, though pretenses
for evil ways are fair, yet these divine principles are as a weight

upon these spirits that carries the soul still towards God. When all is said that can be against God's ways, and in favor of sinful ways, it will, it cannot but hold the conclusion that surely God's ways are good. As a blessed martyr said, "I cannot dispute for the truth, but I can die for the truth." These principles cause if not a disputative knowledge, yet a savory knowledge.

Try to persuade a man by most subtle arguments, eloquent orations, that what he tastes sweet is bitter. Perhaps he cannot answer all you say, but yet he knows the thing is sweet. So the spirit principled rightly with grace, having the savor of the knowledge, as the apostle speaks, though many subtle wiles of Satan and eloquent persuasions from the wisdom of the flesh are brought to persuade to the contrary, yet still it says, "It is good to walk in the ways of godliness."

Every life has principles according to the nature of it, receiving to itself things suitable, or turning from things disagreeable to it; the vegetative life according to the nature of it, so the sensitive, and the rational life, and the life of grace according to it. Most men's spirits are led by the principles of a sensitive life. Few live so high as rational principles reach to. There is a death of the soul in this respect. Only God puts in by a common work of His Spirit some common notions that appear in some, which give but a glimmering light and are very weak. But where the life of grace is in any soul, there are principles of a higher nature, full of light and beauty, carrying the soul to high, spiritual, supernatural things, for the attaining to and enjoyment of the highest good. Other creatures, living at a level under the rational, are made for the enjoyment of no higher good than is within the compass of their own natures, and therefore their principles are only to receive in such good things as are suitable to their natures; and in them they rest satisfied.

I say, they cannot enjoy any higher. Indeed, they are of use

too, and were made for that end, that they might be serviceable to some higher good than themselves but this they do not
enjoy. The destruction of their natures is the highest use that
creatures that are above them have of them. But the rational
creature was made for a higher good than is within the compass
of its own nature, and is intended to enjoy this; and the fuller it
enjoys it, the more perfected it is. Now then, there are required
principles of life accordingly to carry these creatures higher
than their own natures, to have the fruition of that good they
were made for, and to be blessed in the enjoyment of it. Now
these are the principles of grace with which this other spirit is
endued, higher above the principles of reason than the principles of reason are above the principles of sense and thus it is
another spirit.

Second, this other spirit works by another rule. Everything
is guided to its end by some rule that is a beam of God's wisdom. No unreasonable creature knows either its end or rule,
but is acted upon by God to that for which it was made. But the
reasonable creature is of such a nature that it is capable of the
knowledge of both, and therefore cannot be happy without the
knowledge of both and working accordingly. Now it is a great
mercy not to err in the rule that leads to eternal life, to see it,
and act by it. Most of the world makes a mistake here. Their spirits are led by false rulers. They go according to sense, according
to their own carnal apprehension of things, according to their
own wills. They would have the rule of their actions be from
their own spirits or else, Ephesians 2:2, "according to the common course of the world." That which men bless themselves in
is that in which they go, and their living according to the common course is one of the most apparent arguments there is that
yet they are strangers to the way of life; but the godly make the
Word their rule. They look up to the mind of God to see the

beam of divine wisdom let down from heaven to guide them in their way. They look to it for direction, give themselves up to it, dare venture their comforts, estates, safeties, and souls upon it. Psalm 73:24: "Thou shalt guide me by Thy counsel," says David, "and so bring me to Thy glory."

A godly man thinks it a most dishonorable thing to make the example of men his rules. It is for beasts to follow the herd. Examples of men cannot satisfy his conscience. A godly man works for eternity and, therefore, is careful to work by rule. When a man works in a work that concerns his life, he erects a frame that must be for continuance. He makes sure of his rule and often lays his rule to his work. When God erected the frame of the world, which was to last but for a few years, He made all by weight and measure. The frame of man's actions here must be for eternity, and therefore a godly man dares venture upon no other rule but that which is divine. He looks at the Word, not only at the notions of it, and that excellency and beauty he sees in it shining a great way off, but as a light to his feet, and a lantern to his steps. He holds it close to his feet to guide him in his going, knowing that every step he goes is either to hell or heaven. And, doing this, he may look up with comfort for that blessing of God upon His servants. 1 Samuel 2:9: "He keeps the feet of His saints." His way is like the way of the mariner, guided by the heavens.

Third, it is "another spirit," that is, employed about other things. It is not for mean, base services, but is set on working about high and honorable employments. Men of place and dignity have, or ought to have, other spirits differing from ordinary spirits. They cannot endure to be employed in mean and dishonorable works. No, those are fit for mean, base spirits. While other men's spirits are busied about low, poor things and are content in these, minding nothing higher, they are busied about great affairs of state, the high things of the kingdom, consultations about, and transactions of, the great business of the Commonwealth. It was the baseness and dishonor of Domitian's spirit, who, though a great emperor, yet busied himself and spent a great part of his time catching flies; and so of Artaxerxes' spirit, who spent a great deal of time in making halves of knives in a box.

Thus godly men account it too mean a thing for their spirits to be busied about low, base employments. While the spirits of other men are busied about meat, drink, clothes, play, money, lust, and are taken up in these poor things, the spirits of the godly are taken up in the contemplation of the glory of the blessed God, the beauty and high excellency of Jesus Christ, the great counsels of God in the greatest work that He ever did, the work of man's redemption, the great mysteries of the gospel, the glorious things of the kingdom of Jesus Christ, the great things of eternity, the interest they have in all the good in God, Christ, heaven, about setting out the glory of the blessed God in the world, lifting up His name, working together with God in glorying Himself, observing God's ways in His glorious works of creation and providence, preparing and fitting themselves for the glorious appearing of the great God, joining with those blessed creatures, the angels and saints in heaven, magnifying, praising, worshipping and adoring the Lord of all. These are things fit for the spirits of the godly; they are not suitable to the spirits of the world. As Psalm 92:6 says: "A brutish man knows not, neither doth a fool understand this."

A godly man may be busied in mean, low things, but his spirit will not be content, nor taken up, nor satisfied in those things as adequate objects for him as the spirits of the world are. They are objects adequate to any principles they have. A man who is understanding may sometimes condescend to sport with children in low things, but these do not take up his spirit as adequate objects for what he has in himself. If, indeed, he should find contentment and satisfaction in such things, it would argue a childish spirit in him. So it is here.

Fourth, this spirit is carried to other ends. The spirit of the world looks at ease, pleasure, honor, gain, and self in all. It is a low spirit in an ill sense. It subjects not only ordinary actions, but the best things it does, even the duties of God's worship, to base, low, unworthy ends. At the highest point, the most excellent of the heathens, who had the most brave spirits the world had in their time, aimed no higher than to work according to reason, to satisfy the dictates of rational principles and a natural conscience. They did not know what it was to honor God, to aim at God in all they did. But the spirit of the godly is a raised spirit. It looks at God and eternity in all it does. It carries things up to the highest good and wrestles until it gets through all creatures and closes with God. It accounts the excellency of what it is and what it has to be for God, and directs what it does to Him, and in this comes as near the working of God Himself, and works as much like Him as is possible.

It is the glory of God to be the first cause and last end, and to work *from* Himself and *for* Himself. No creature can work from itself, but as it has its principle from God so it works for Him, giving Him the glory as the first cause and last end. And this is the great worship that God has from His creature, both in this world and eternally in heaven.

We speak much of honoring, serving, and worshipping God. We do nothing unless we do this. God made the world so that He might have some creatures to make Him the highest and last end of all. Many who have excellent natural parts are often busied about deeper things than other men, but, their spirits being corrupt, they are not carried to God in all that they do. They dive deep, but all comes to nothing. They are like children diving deep in the water who bring up nothing but shells and gravel.

1. Now where the spirit is carried to God as the last end, there, first, the beauty, excellency, and glory of whatever it has or does are judged according to the reference it has to God. It is true, I have these mercies. I do such and such things, but is God honored by all? All things are as dead to this spirit where it does not see God's name lifted up and so the excellency; and beauty of what others have or do, if God is not honored by them, it looks on them as dead things.

2. All it has, is, or does lies in an absolute subjection under God to be at His disposal. All things are absolutely subject to the last end.

3. Where God is aimed at as the highest end, there God's glory is willed infinitely; no limit, no bounds are set to the desires or endeavors of the soul after it.

This spirit has other qualifications. The spirit of the godly is glorious within.

*First, it is an enlightened spirit.* The light of the glory of God in the face of Jesus Christ has shined into it and transformed it into the same image (2 Corinthians 4:6). In Daniel 5:11, they said that Daniel was a man in whom the Spirit of the holy God was because light, understanding, and wisdom were found in him. Surely, the Spirit of the living God is here because light, understanding, and wisdom are found here. This is the true light, the light of life that has a quickening power and influence of life in it. There is a great difference between the light of the sun shining in a garden and the light of torches. There is the influence of an enlivening power in the one and not in the other. Such difference there is between the light in the spirits of the wicked men and the light in the spirits of the godly. It is the knowledge of the holy that is true understanding (Proverbs 9:10). And a man of such understanding is of an excellent spirit indeed, (Proverbs 17:27). This is that which the Holy Ghost calls spiritual understanding (Colossians 1:9), to distinguish it from that understanding which is in natural men. They see into spiritual things after another manner than other men. They see the reality, beauty, excellency, and glory of those things that are hidden from drossy, vile spirits. The gospel is said to be a mystery revealed unto the saints (Colossians 1:26). The law and testimonies are sealed and bound up among the disciples. The Lord delighted to reveal Himself to men of excellent spirits, who are only fit to close with divine and spiritual truths. As none can teach as God teaches (Job 36:22), so none knows the things of God as the godly do. They behold Him with open face. They walk on in the light of the face of God (Psalm 89:15). Their spirits are elevated by such a light as is suitable to that light which is in God Himself and that luster of His image that shines in the face of Jesus Christ. But the spirit of the world is a spirit of darkness; even that light which is in them is darkness.

*Second, it is a free spirit.* Psalm 51:12: "Establish me with Thy free spirit." And this freedom makes it indeed a true, royal, princely spirit, for so the word signifies that is translated in that place "a free spirit." The words are "Establish me with Thy royal, princely spirit."

It is a free, disengaged spirit, not entangled or ensnared with base, earthly engagements like the spirits of the world. It is a spirit that is at liberty. "Where the Spirit of the Lord is, there is liberty" (2 Corinthians 3:17). How the engagements of worldly spirits miserably enthrall them, that notwithstanding convictions of conscience, notwithstanding much unquietness of their hearts in their way, many checks, secret wounds of spirit, sinking damps and fears, yet they cannot get their hearts off from those engagements they are so miserably, so dangerously entangled in! This is a woeful bondage. Those who are godly can remember a time when their hearts were thus ensnared, but it was the blessed work of the Lord to set them at liberty; and now they have ease; now they have sweet quiet and rest for their spirits.

It is free from the bondage of sin, not under the power and command of it. It has command over itself, over its passions; not in a base slavery to Satan, not in servile subjection to men, not brought under the power of any creature. It was a notable free expression of two blessed martyrs, Surgius and Bacchus, who were two great courtiers being accused of being Christians and commanded to offer sacrifice unto the idols. They refused to go to the temple, and gave this answer to the Emperor: "We, O Emperor, are bound unto you only in an earthly warfare. You have no right over our souls. God only will be Lord of them." It will not be forced to do anything that is base. God leaves the body and estates of His servants to the power of men oftentimes, but their spirits are free. It is too base a disposition of a servant of God to plead necessity of sinning. No creature can compel another to sin. Tertullian has an excellent expression to this purpose. The state of faith does not admit alleging a necessity of sinning in dealing with those whom the only necessity is not to offend.

It is free with regard to slavish fear. It is able to look upon the face of God with joy. Job 22:26: "Thou shalt have delight in the Almighty, and shall lift up thy face to God." The Scripture speaks of a spirit of fear and a spirit of bondage from both of which this spirit is set at liberty. It can look upon the power, sovereignty, justice, and holiness of God and rejoice in them, glad that God is so holy and just and that it has to deal with such a God. It has access to His presence with boldness and liberty of speech (Ephesians 3:12), as the word signifies there. It has sweet and blessed freedom in the performance of holy duties. It is not forced and hauled to them; it does not take them up as tiresome burdens. God's commandments are not grievous. They are not as fetters of iron, but as chains of gold for beauty and ornament. There is a readiness of spirit to whatever good. They are vessels of honor, ready and prepared unto every good work (2 Timothy 2:21). "It is written in the volume of thy book that I should do thy will, and lo, I come" (Psalm 40:7–8). There is a suitableness between the law and the spirit. The law is written in it, never so much in its element as when it is in the ways of obedience. There is not the straitness of spirit as in others, but here the heart sweetly enlarges itself as the flower that opens itself to the shining of the sun.

*Third, it is a sublime spirit raised high by spiritual, heavenly influences, not swelling by pride.* It is a spirit that has all earthly things under its feet, as the Holy Ghost sets out the church (Revelation 12:1). It looks with contempt on things received with admiration by other spirits as being infinitely inferior to it. A godly man's feet are where other men's heads are; the other men's heads being the pitch and height of all their aims, are upon things that are on the earth, but the saints have these things under their feet.

When Valence sent to offer Basil great preferments, to tell him what a great man he might be, Basil answered, "Offer these things to children, not to Christians." When some tried to stop Luther's mouth with preferments, one of his adversaries answered, "It is in vain, he cares not for gold." His spirit was too noble and high to be tempted with gold. Base, low spirits would have been taken with such things. Such a spirit was Demas, who forsook Paul to embrace this present world; but a spirit raised by God is above them.

How was St. Paul's spirit above money? When he speaks of lucre, he calls it "filthy lucre" (1 Timothy 3:3). A godly man's spirit is suitable to the high dignities put upon it and the privileges it has. Saul, when made a king, had another spirit put upon him, condemning former things highly esteemed. A man raised on high looks on things below, and they appear small things to him. So it is here. Reason may raise the spirits of men above the common sort. A rational man looks at many sins as too mean and base for him, scorns to stain his excellency with them, as the sins of sensuality and filthy lusts. Tertullian thinks him not worthy the name of a man who spends a whole day in the pleasures of the flesh. Socrates had such a vile esteem of sin that he thought it shall be one of the greatest torments of men in another life to be tied and bound to the sins they most delighted in here. Seneca has a notable expression to this purpose: "I am too great, and born to greater things, than that I should be a slave to my body."

But if reason raises the spirit so high, how high, then, does grace raise it? This spirit cannot be satisfied with small, low things. It is reported of Luther that when great gifts were sent to him he refused them with this most brave and excellent speech: "I did earnestly protest that God should not put me off with these things," meaning that he would not be satisfied with any things that were here below. All the things in the world are far from being able to satisfy this spirit. It accounts all, yea, if they were a thousand times more than they are, but a poor pittance for the portion of an immortal soul. If God should make more worlds for it, yet if He does not give Himself to it, it would not be satisfied. Nothing but a God, an infinite, universal, eternal good, can fill up the desires of this spirit. "Thou hast made us, O Lord, for thyself," says Augustine, "and our hearts are unquiet till they come unto thee."

It is the work of a base, drossy spirit to think, "If I had but so much, or so much yearly, I should have enough." How base the spirit of that rich man, blessing himself in his goods, Luke 12:19: "Soul, take thine ease, thou hast goods laid up for many years." What were all those to his soul, to the happiness of his soul? These are spirits that have higher designs than so. Their designs are no less than a kingdom, yea, than God Himself. Romans 2:7: "They seek for glory, honor, immortality, eternal life." Though they can be content with little of the world for their use, yet they cannot be content without that good and happiness that is infinitely higher and better than all the world for their portion. As Abraham said concerning his child, when God promised him a great reward, Genesis 15:2: "Lord, what wilt thou give me, so long as I go childless?" As if he were to say, "Lord, what is all the reward I can have, unless I have this mercy, unless I have a child?" He said this because the Messiah was to come out of his loins.

So the soul is here. If God should promise it never such great things, yet, "Lord, what are all these things to me if I do not have You?" All the gifts that God can give to this spirit will not satisfy it unless He gives Himself to it. As God is not pleased with what we tender to Him unless we give ourselves to Him, so a godly heart is not contented with all that God gives to it unless He gives Himself to it. Thus Bernard said exceedingly sweetly, "As what I have, if offered to Thee, pleaseth not Thee, O Lord, without myself; so the good things we have from Thee, though they may refresh us, yet they satisfy us not without Thyself."

Yea, further, the enjoyment of God is not enough unless they may have a full enjoyment of Him. They are not satisfied unless they are filled with the fullness, yea, with all the fullness of God (Ephesians 3:19). See a notable example of this in Moses beginning at Exodus 33:12. The Lord had done great things for Moses in many ways; but besides all He had done for him He told him that He knew him by name and that he had found favor in His sight. One would have thought that this might have satisfied him. No, Moses must have more, verse 13: "I pray Thee, if I have found grace in Thy sight, show me Thy way, that I may know Thee, and that I may find grace in Thy sight." God granted him this and told him, verse 14, that His presence shall go with him and He will give him rest. Surely this will satisfy him! No, verse 16, Moses must have more. He must have such a presence as the world may know that God goes with him, and that he and his people are separated people from all the people that are upon the face of the earth.

In verse 17, the Lord said to him, "I will give thee this thing also that thou hast spoken." Surely this will satisfy him. No, Moses is not satisfied yet. Verse 18: "I beseech Thee, show me Thy glory." He must have more of God yet. God grants him this also, verse 19: "I will make all My goodness pass before thee." And so the Lord passed by him and proclaimed His great and glorious name before him. He showed Moses as much of His glory as he was able to behold. Surely Moses had enough now. No, not yet (chapter 34:9). God must pardon the sin of his people, too, and take him and them for His inheritance. He must have this fruit of God's favor higher than all the rest. See how, as we may so say with holy reverence, he encroached, as it were, upon God as one who could never have enough, and yet God liked this exceedingly well! Here is a spirit, indeed, that is not satisfied with mean and ordinary things. In a spiritual sense, the godly seek great things for themselves, and it is their glory to do so. God delights to have the spirits of His children thus raised. He would not have them to be of such sordid spirits as to mind no higher things than the base drudges of the world do. A prince or nobleman delights to see the spirit of his child raised to a higher degree than the ordinary sort of men.

*Fourth, it is a firm, strong spirit.* Isaiah 11:2: the Spirit of Christ is a spirit of might: first, strong to resist strong temptations; second, strong to overcome strong corruptions; third, strong to bear strong afflictions.

First, it is not every temptation that can prevail with these. Little things will draw weak, childish spirits; but such temptations as others do not know how to resist, these can stand before them and go on in their way without any alteration of spirit by them. Though they live in the midst of temptations, yet they are able to keep themselves unspotted—like the three children who walked in the fire and yet the smell of the fire came not upon them nor their garments, or like the children of Israel who walked on the dry land safely with the seas on each side of them. They are ashamed to complain of temptations, to excuse themselves by their temptations; for what reason has the work of God been so mighty upon their spirits but to strengthen them against temptations? Many temptations, which others think to be strong, they scarcely take notice of, so far are their spirits above them.

Luther was so far above the sin of covetousness that he said of himself that he found no temptations to that sin, though his spirit was very pestered with temptations of other kinds. The devil will not set upon such with ordinary temptations. He knows it is in vain. When he comes upon them, it is with temptations of a higher nature, of stronger efficacy.

You know that some men's bodies are of such strong constitutions that that which will work mightily upon others will not stir them. So it is with men's spirits. The devil does not need to trouble himself about many. The poorest, slightest temptations are enough to draw them to what he would have. Yes, and as those who account themselves to be brave, of more than ordinary spirits, who can stand out strongly against God and His truth—the strongest arguments, the drawing motives, the powerful persuasions of the Word do not move them at all. But every poor temptation of the devil draws them any way. They have no power to resist but are led as the ox to the slaughter and the fool to the stocks. The godly man is strong in the Lord and in the power of His might (Ephesians 6:10). Other men are strong in their lusts, and in the power of them against the Lord and His truth.

Second, they can overcome strong corruptions. Temptations from without do not have as much power as corruptions that are within. Yet when these rise up like a flood, "The Spirit of the Lord in them sets up a standard against them" (Isaiah 59:19). Yea, by a contrary stream, this Spirit opposes and overcomes them. The more suitable any corruption is to the natural disposition, the more powerfully it has heretofore prevailed, the more strongly it would now put forth itself, the more this spirit keeps it under control above all others.

Every ordinary spirit can oppose and is able to resist some mean, contemptible sin that brings little pleasure or profit with it. When sin is, as it were, weakened and numbed by afflictions, then they can cast it off. When the strength of it is abated for lack of fuel, for lack of opportunity to act upon it, for lack of bodily strength to put it forth, then they can leave their sin. Simeon and Levi came upon the Shechemites when they were sore and overcame them. So they can come upon their sin in times of affliction and overcome it, and this they think to be repentance, which is a mistake. But this spirit can oppose sin when it is vigorous, strong, and active, and overcome it.

Let God put this spirit into one who is young and strong, whose bones are full of marrow, who has the world to smile on him and may have opportunities to fully enjoy his lust. Yet now he shall be able to overcome his corruption and prevail against the strongest lust. As it is said of Moses in Hebrews 11:24, "When he was full of years," he then could deny himself and refuse the pleasures of the flesh. The word in the original is "when he was great," when he was grown up to ripeness, when he might have enjoyed his pleasure to the fullest. Yet now he was able to overcome himself and the world, and this required strength of spirit, indeed.

Third, it is strong to bear strong afflictions. In that sense it is like a strong man who can endure cold, harsh weather which others would scarcely put their heads out into. Such difference is there in the spirits of men with regard to their bearing afflictions. Some are always complaining, murmuring, and whining at every little affliction. Their hearts fret, vex, and rage under it. For some men, if their flesh is but scratched with a pin, it immediately festers and rankles. In Job 23:2 he says his stroke was heavier than his groaning; but these men's groanings are heavier than their strokes. They are like rotten boughs of trees. If a little weight is hung on them, they immediately break. A little thing will break the spirits of these men; a little thing will cause them to sink and pine away, and put them in a desperate sullenness to make away themselves. "If thou faintest in adversity thy strength is small," said Solomon in Proverbs 24:10.

What poor things are they that many men's spirits are unable to bear! Not a frown from a great man, not a conceit of the least disparagement that they suffer in anything; these are but toys and trifles which a man of an excellent spirit would scorn to even bestow a thought about, like the loss of a little money. I have read of one who hung himself because he had a dream that he had lost his money. Others, if they meet with but a little disturbance in their family from husbands and wives, if their parents but cross them, if their hopes are frustrated in things of no great importance, they cannot bear it. They sink down in such desperate discouragements that their lives are bitter to them. They are weary of them and seek to ease themselves by putting an end to their lives. Impatient, sinking desperateness always proceeds from a base weakness of spirit. Despair is an exceedingly vile and contemptible sin. Gulielmus Parisiensis, speaking of despair, had this expression, "I despair! Oh, word of eternal reproach and confusion, of dishonor never to be blotted out! It publishes the devil to be the conqueror and would thou didst see the devil crowned as a conqueror whom thou dost so shamefully lie under."

These sinking, sullen-spirited people may please themselves in the froward distempers of their hearts and conceit, as if they were fruits of humility, but let them know that the devil is the most sullen spirit there is, and yet the most proud. Though in your frowardness you fly from God and let your spirit sink down even as low as the bottom of the sea, yet even there the wrath of God will follow you. As it says in Amos 9:3, "Though they hide themselves in the bottom of the sea I will command the serpent to bite them."

Thus those whose spirits are sunk into the bottom of the sea of desperation shall have no ease there. Even there the Lord will command the serpent to bite them. The devil shall vex and torment them there. Many, while in their prosperity, while the world smiles on them, seem to be of brave and stout spirits. To be sure, they are scornful, proud, and high. They are all for mirth and jollity. They are so afraid of sadness that they banish all seriousness. But when affliction comes upon these, when God touches them with sickness, what poor spirits are they then! How their hearts sink like lead! How disconsolate! How dejected are they then!

Manasseh was of a bold, presumptuous spirit, and was exceedingly scornful in the time of his prosperity. He went on with a high hand against God, as if he meant to contest with heaven itself. But mark what is in 2 Chronicles 33:11, when he was brought into trouble what a poor, base spirit he had. He ran among the thorns; he hid himself in the bushes and from there he was taken and bound in fetters. As it was said of Alexander, it was nothing for him to carry himself bravely because he always conquered, but for Caesar to behave himself wisely and to uphold his spirit when he was conquered and others fainted, this was high praise to him. You talk of merry hearts and joyful spirits, but can you be joyful in affliction? Will your spirits hold out in tribulation? Can you rejoice in the greatest troubles? Will your comforts hold out in sore and grievous distresses? This would be a sign of strength of spirit, indeed! The spirit of a man can sustain his infirmities, said Solomon. This is the strength of a man's spirit—to be able to carry itself bravely and undauntedly in the midst of the greatest afflictions. Your spirits can bear nothing; they are childish, poor, weak spirits, not to be accounted the spirits of men. Lactantius boasts of the bravery of the spirits of the martyrs in his time in this respect: "Our children and women (not to speak of our men), in silence, overcome their tormentors, and the fire cannot fetch so much as a sigh from them."

*Fifth, they are generous spirits:* 1. They are not mercenary. They will not make deals with God for what they do, only doing as much as they must to get their money and no more. No, they go on in their work and leave themselves to God. Let the benefit of what they do be what it will, they do not lose their end if they are employed for God. Men do very ill for themselves in engaging with God for any service, for their strait spirits cannot imagine or desire that latitude of good that the infinite bounty of God would give if they left themselves wholly to it.

Seneca proves the opinion of such who said a man should

choose a friend that he might have one, who might relieve him in want and visit him in his sickness. "No," said he, "this is mercenary. I will choose a friend that I may have one to show love to, to visit if he is sick, to help if he is in need."

So for men to choose a God unto themselves that they may be helped out of troubles, that they may have their estates blessed, that they may get such and such things by Him to make this the highest end is mercenary and too low for a true, gracious, generous spirit. But to choose a God to be my God that I may honor, love, fear, and worship Him forever, this is true Christian generosity.

2. A true, generous spirit cannot endure basely to subject itself to any, that is, to flatter and fawn and be serviceable to men's lusts and base humor for advantage's sake. It knows how to lie under the feet of any to do them good where God may have honor. But to be a servant to any man's lust whatever it cannot endure. We read that those who flattered Dionysius were so gross in their flatteries that when he spat they licked up his spittle and said, "It is sweeter than nectar and ambrosia." It is likewise reported of Cambyses that, falling in love with his sister, he asked the judges whether it was lawful for him to marry her. They answered that they had no such law, but they had another that the king could do whatever pleased him, whereupon he married her. Such base-spiritedness cannot stand with Christian generosity.

3. A true, generous spirit is not ready to take advantage of those who are under it. Men of these spirits love to pity and relieve those whom they have advantage over, as did Elisha in 2 Kings 6:22–23. When he had the Syrians in the midst of Samaria and the king of Israel asked him, "Shall I smite them? Shall I smite them?" He answered, "Thou shalt not smite them; set bread and water before them that they may eat and drink

and go to their master: and he prepared great provision for them, and when they had eaten and drunk, he sent them away." It is reported that the lion spares those things that fall down and submit to it, but the wolf, the bear, and the dog rend and tear what they get hold of. To be able to do someone hurt and not do it is truly noble. It is the glory of a King, yes, of God Himself, to pass by an offense. To show mercy, said Chrysostom, is a more glorious thing than to raise the dead, and a greater work than to build the most magnificent temples.

Many base-spirited men, who will crouch low enough to those who are above them, are yet imperious, cruel, hardhearted, rugged, fierce towards those that are under them, and they think it the bravery and greatness of their spirits that they can insult those under them and avenge themselves upon them. But there is nothing great in these men but pride and self-love. This is the greatest baseness of spirit that can be, and the more these men formerly revealed their baseness, in their sordid crouchings unto others who were above them, the more do they now reveal the vileness of their spirits in their cruel insults of those who are under them. And this they think is a good and brave thing, that they can trample upon others, whereas the kindness of a man is the goodness, beauty, and excellency of a man's spirit. The word in Isaiah 40:6 that is translated "the goodliness of the flower" is the same word which signifies kindness. We read in Revelation 9 that the locusts that came out of the smoking pit had faces as the faces of men, and they had hair as the hair of women. They had fair countenances. They could look smiling and flattering upon men for their own ends, but their teeth were the teeth of lions, and they had tails like scorpions to tear and sting those over whom they had an advantage. An insulting spirit toward those over whom we have an advantage is far from true generosity, however men may bless themselves in it.

Rehoboam was a man of an exceedingly imperious, insulting disposition. "My little finger," said he, "shall be thicker than my father's loins; my father put a heavy yoke upon you, but I will put more to your yoke; my father chastised you with whips, but I will chastise you with scorpions." Oh, what a spirit was here! Surely he, and those who put him on, rejoiced in this as a brave, commanding spirit indeed! But the Holy Ghost said that Rehoboam was a poor, weak, childish-spirited man. Yes, He calls him a child though he was over forty years old (2 Chronicles 13:7). "He was young," the text says; but the word is that used of a tender-hearted child who is, of a poor, soft, effeminate spirit. True generosity and cruelty are exceedingly opposed to one another; one destroys the other. When David's spirit was distempered, when he had lost much of his generosity by that sin of uncleanness, Psalm 51, where he prays to God for His free spirit, where the word signifies a royal, princely spirit, as I noted before, much of the royal princeliness of his spirit was lost by that sin. And David was never so rigid as he was at this time, which appears in 2 Samuel 12:30–31 where he commanded the people whom he had overcome to be brought forth. He put them under saws and harrows of iron and made them pass through the brick kiln, and thus did he unto all the cities of the children of Ammon. This was very harsh and rigid. We never read that he ever dealt this way with any before.

Now it is observable that this act of his was at the time wherein he laid in his sin. For Joab had besieged that city before David saw Bathsheba, and it was at that siege where Uriah was slain. And although this fact was related after Nathan came to him, after Solomon's birth, it is probable that it was before, even while he lay in his sin, for two reasons:

First, because it is not probable that the siege continued

not only till the child conceived in adultery was born, but after the birth of Solomon, too, as it here stands in the story.

Second, it is not likely that David, having newly received mercy from God as he did in the pardon of his sin, and when his heart was so broken as it was, would then show such rigid severity only for the abuse of his messengers. The reason why this is set after is that, in the time of the siege, David committed the adultery, and so the whole story concerning David and Bathsheba is first related, and then he comes to the story of the war again.

4. A generous spirit is studious and diligent to return good as well as desirous to receive good, as David in Psalm 116:12: "What shall I render unto the Lord?" said he. He speaks as a man pressed in his spirit, troubled until he returned something. He accounts favors received as obligations as great as any debts in the world. It is infinite baseness in spirit to be so for oneself that, if one's own turn is served, then neither God nor man is regarded. How many men will crouch and yield to anything till they have gotten their own turns served; but then they grow proud and regard less those, yea, are oftentimes spiteful against those, to whom (when time was) they crouched for favors, and from whom they received many by which they came to that which now they are.

A notable example of this we have in Benhadad, king of Syria. In 1 Kings 20:32, he caused his servants to gird themselves with sackcloth on their loins, put ropes on their heads, and to come to the king of Israel and say, "Thy servant Benhadad saith, 'I pray thee, let me live' "; and he was content to yield to any terms when the king of Israel had him at advantage. Verse 34: "The cities which my father took from thy father, I will restore, and then shalt make streets for thee in Damascus." But later, when Ahab was ready to go to war with him to get those cities (chapter 22:3), observe the baseness of the spirit of

Benhadad. He who before had so crouched to Ahab for his life now commanded his captains to fight neither with small nor great, save only with the king of Israel (1 Kings 22:31). See with what malice he sought the life of him who before had saved his.

5. A generous spirit loves to be abundant in service. It is not satisfied in doing mean and ordinary things. Before they were sublime in that. Receiving ordinary things from God would not satisfy them, but they must have great things from him. So now it is their generosity. They will not be quieted in doing ordinary things for God, but they must do great things for Him. They prize their service as well as their wages, as in John 17:4. Christ said that He had finished the work that His Father gave Him to do. He accounted His work a gift. Thus those who have the Spirit of Christ account their services to be gifts from God. To live unserviceably they would account to be the greatest burden in the world to them. They would rather have less comforts and more service than more comforts and less service. They would rather be straitened in comforts than in duties. To what purpose do we live if we are of no use? It is the baseness of men's spirits (which a truly godly man abhors) when men desire to receive great things but are content in doing little. They put off God with ordinary, slight services; but the spirits of the saints are more generous than this. If it were possible they would be infinite in service to God. They never think they have done enough for Him. "I will yet praise Thee more and more," said David in Psalm 71:14. "I will add to Thy praise"; so the words are in the original. As if he should say, "God has had some praise in the world already; I would fain add something for my part. I would come in with my share, that He might have some more praise from me." And this not an ordinary praise, but he endeavors to have the high praises of God in heart and mouth (Psalm

149:6). He desires to make the praise of God glorious (Psalm 66:2). He would fain be eminent in good works. Titus 3:14: "Let ours also learn to maintain good works." The words are, "Let them learn to be eminent in good works above others."

There is a holy ambition in them to get above others in godliness. This is, indeed, to walk circumspectly, to which the apostle exhorts us in Ephesians 5:15. The word there translated "circumspectly" signifies to get up to the top of godliness, to perfect holiness in the fear of God; and therefore he sets the highest pitch of the rule before him. He would not have the rule come down to him, but he endeavors to get up to the rule. He sets before himself the highest examples he can. He is not willing to offer to God that which costs him nothing, but if there is anything more choice, more excellent, or better than others, it shall be for God. He loves to be abundant in duty. He would not scant God, to give only that which he must of necessity, but loves to be fruitful in all good works.

The reasonings of many men's spirits show much baseness in them: "Why are we bound to do this? Is it absolutely necessary? Cannot a man be saved unless he does this? May not such a thing be lawfully done?"

If you had a raised, generous spirit for God, it would be enough to you that such a thing is good, is commendable, or may be serviceable: "If God may have glory by it, I may do good by it; and if such a thing has no excellency in it, God shall have no glory by it." This would be enough to cause the soul greedily and delightfully to embrace the one and freely and strongly to reject the other.

A generous spirit strives to be abundant in doing good and leaves itself with God, let God do with him what seems good in His eyes. It does not maintain jealous, suspicious thoughts of God, as if it were best to provide for itself and not dare to venture upon God. Base, unworthy spirits reveal themselves much in this. They will part with nothing, but first will see what they shall have. They must have present pay and be sure it is in their hand. They are jealous and suspicious of everyone. They are conscious to themselves of baseness this way, and therefore look upon all others as if they were only for themselves too.

But a generous spirit finds in itself a disposition ready to do good to others, though they can do little for him. Yet if they need and are able, he finds he can freely and readily do it. And this makes him venture upon others so that they will likewise, out of freedom and generosity, be helpful to him if occasion and need serve, though they should not receive recompense from him. And therefore he is not ready to entertain jealous and suspicious thoughts, as other baser spirits do.

Thus, with respect to God, he knows God is infinitely good and blessed in Himself; and that He, out of His own infinite goodness, is ready to do good and help those in want, who are able to do little again in way of requital; but that He, for His name's sake, shows mercy and loving kindness to His poor creatures because mercy pleases Him. And therefore he can venture himself upon God.

As base spirits are very jealous with regard to trust, so they are very suspicious of love. They think (because they are conscious of unworthiness, and that they love only their own ends) they cannot be truly beloved of others but so far as they are useful to them. But one of a generous spirit knows in himself that he can love others not only because he receives good from them, but that he may do good to them. Therefore he sees this to be infinitely more in God, and therefore he can rely upon God's love in spite of his own unworthiness. Though the Lord can receive no good from me, yet he can do good unto me. And this, I believe, is the glorious excellency of the Lord, and therefore my spirit shall not give way to suspicious thoughts of His love.

David says in 2 Samuel 23:5, "Although my house be not so with God, yet He hath made me an everlasting covenant ordered in all things, and sure; for this is all my salvation, and all my desire, although He maketh it not to grow." And it is observable that it is said of him in verse 1 that when he spoke this, he was a man who was raised up on high. It is true even in this sense, that that expression of his in verse 5 was an argument of a man whose spirit was truly raised on high. And the rather does a generous spirit abandon base, jealous, suspicious thoughts of God's faithfulness and love because it knows in itself that it has not such a vile disposition as to abuse this gracious and blessed nature that it apprehends of God so as to be the more secure and loose, to give liberty to itself in any evil, because of this. Oh, no! God forbid! This is so far from a true generous spirit—this spirit of baseness, this sordid disposition—indeed that it loathes, it abhors the thought of it. It finds in itself that the sight of this grace of God, this blessed nature of God, draws it most sweetly to Him to close with Him, to delight in Him. It is the strongest motive to draw it up to holiness, yea, to "perfect holiness in the fear of God" (2 Corinthians 7:1). And therefore it calls out jealous and suspicious thoughts of the goodness and love of the blessed God as fruits of baseness of spirit.

6. Though sublime and raised as before, yet withal it is a humble, broken, and contrite spirit, one who is poor in spirit. This is a blessed conjunction indeed. It thinks itself too good for any lust, yet not too good to subject itself to the least commandment. Though it will not be under the power of any creature, yet it will lie flat and trembling under the least word of the Lord (Isaiah 66:2). Though it is not satisfied with mean things, yet it accounts itself less then the least of all God's mercies. How sublime was Paul's spirit when he accounted all things dung, yet he

himself could be content to be accounted an off-scouring for Christ. The sublimity of his spirit was not a greater glory to him in the one than the humility of it was in the other. Though a godly man minds high things above others, yet he can be well content to be used in the meanest services for the good of others. Though he is raised above the world, yet he judges himself less than the least of the saints. Though he aims at the highest pitch of godliness, yet he blesses God for, and makes much of, the least breathings of His Spirit. And such a heart is precious indeed in God's eyes. "This, O Lord, Thou canst not despise" (Psalm 51:17). God can despise kings and emperors. God can despise the glory and luster of the world, but a humble, broken spirit the Lord cannot despise. There is no object that God accounts worth looking at in the world but such a one (Isaiah 66:2). "To him will I look," says God. The highest heavens and the lowest heart are the two places of God's most glorious residence.

7. It is a public spirit, enlarged for public good; not a narrow base, straitened spirit. Godliness mightily enlarges the heart of man. The Lord persuaded Japheth to dwell in the tents of Shem. The words in Genesis 9:27 signify, "The Lord shall enlarge the *heart* of Japheth." When a man is converted, his heart is converted and his heart is enlarged. And it must be so, for now the Spirit makes the enjoyment of God an infinite, universal good. Now it opens itself to receive and embrace a God in whom it expects all good. Before it followed after some poor drops of good in the creature, but now finds all is to be enjoyed in God Himself. And, being thus enlarged to receive a universal good, it desires to enlarge itself as much as it can to be a universal good, but that is proper to God. Yet a public good it may be, and therefore it spreads itself as far as it can. Now it loves good as good, not upon particular private grounds; and

therefore the more good, the more beloved. It minds good as in reference to God; and therefore, where God may be most honored, there the heart is most solicitous, most industrious. It is willing, therefore, to empty itself of its private good that the public may be furthered.

If nature will venture its own particular good for the general (as heavy things will ascend contrary to their natures to keep out vacuity and so to preserve the universe), much more then will grace. Every godly man, one way or another, according to the abilities he has, is a public blessing to the place where he lives. The saints of God are compared to a cloud in Hebrews 12:1. The comparison is true in this respect: a cloud waters the earth as a common blessing. So they are not as waterpots that water but a few spots of ground in a garden.

And this publicness of spirit is then right and truly gracious, first, when it is content to do public good where the person himself shall be taken little notice of. As many times the engine that does all in great works is inward, hidden, and not taken notice of.

Second, when he can be glad that any public good work goes on and prospers, though others are used in it and not himself, to the eclipsing of his light.

Third, when he is willing to be used in any service though but to prepare work for others, which they, not he, shall have the glory of after he is gone. Luther, writing to Melanchthon, encouraged him against the strong opposition that they met with in the cause of God. "God (said he) is able to preserve His own cause falling, and to raise it fallen; if we be not worthy, let it be done by others." Such public spirit as this is an excellent spirit indeed.

8. It is a sanctified spirit. 1 Thessalonians 4:8: "He hath made us partakers of His Holy Spirit." Chapter 5:23: "I pray

God sanctify you throughout, your whole spirit and soul." Sanctified, that is:

First, it is not such a mixed spirit as the common spirit of the world. It does not have that mixture of filth and dross in it but is pure. Purity consists in freedom from mixture with that which is of a baser nature. If mixed with that which is of a superior nature, it does not make the thing itself impure, as when silver is mixed with lead or dross. The spirits of the godly are mixed with grace, but that makes them more excellent and pure. Their spirits close with such mixture of spiritual excellency that is above the excellency of the soul; but if there comes any mixture with that which is base, beneath the excellency of the spirit, this defiles, and this their spirits cannot close with, but are sensible of the evil of it and never stop working till it is purged out.

Second, sanctified in that God has set them apart for Himself. Psalm 4:3: "Know that the Lord hath set apart him that is godly for Himself." And they have devoted, dedicated, and consecrated themselves to and for God. They are spirits resigned and given up to the Lord.

Third, all the parts, abilities, and common gifts of this spirit are sanctified. A higher excellency is put upon them than they have in the spirits of other men. Weak, natural parts in these are more excellent than the strongest not sanctified. As the consecration of wood, leather, and mean things puts greater excellency upon them than gold and silver have that are not so consecrated, yet the larger the natural parts are of a sanctified spirit, the more excellent it is.

Fourth, it is able to make a sanctified use of what it meddles with, of what it has to deal in; of all the works and ways of God, it makes all to be holy to the Lord.

9. It is a true, heroic spirit. None have such brave, heroic

spirits as God's servants have. It is not discouraged by difficulties; it will set upon things a sluggish spirit thinks impossible; it will go through that which such a one thinks can never be; it breaks through armies of difficulties that it might go on in its way and accomplish its work, not discouraged as the sluggish spirit, who cries out, "There is a lion in the way." It is not the difficulty of the work but the baseness of our spirits that ordinarily hinders us in our way. Some difficulties that others count great hindrances it slights and condemns as reproach and scorn in the ways of God. It can condemn condemners and vilify those who account the ways of God as vile. This is the true spirit of Jesus Christ, of whom it is said in Hebrews 12:2, "He endured the cross, and despised the shame." The shame whereby others despised Him was despised *of* Him, who did not account it a thing worthy for His spirit to be troubled at. No more is a true godly spirit hindered on his way by this than one riding on with strength in his journey is hindered by the barking of whippets at his horse's heels. He rides on and minds them not. And as for railings and revilings at the ways of God, by which many are discouraged, the spirit of a godly man can shake them off as Saint Paul did the viper that hung upon his hand and feel no hurt. It bears off many hardships that are likely to be very grievous to flesh and blood, that it is likely to meet with that which discourages the hearts of many, both from beginning to enter upon God's ways and from continuing in them after they have begun.

The spirits of the other spies who were sent with Caleb and Joshua were undaunted. They would go up and possess the land, let whatever could be stand in their way. Thus, many have convictions of conscience that the ways of God indeed are good, but the great hardships that they are likely to suffer in those ways keep them off. But a true godly spirit is willing to embrace religion with all the hard terms annexed unto it. It is a poor, mean spirit that must engage God beforehand: "If I were sure to hold out, to have at last that which I desire, *then* I would venture upon the says of godliness. But I am afraid it will never be." And so it sinks and has no mind to set upon the work.

But *this* spirit will set upon the work with all the hazards like Esther, who said, "If I perish, I perish." This was a brave spirit indeed! What if she had had such a base cowardly spirit as many, so as to think, "Alas, what good shall I do? I may hazard myself, and bring myself into trouble, but no likelihood of any good will come of it"? She is content to venture all upon a mere possibility of good; to break through armies of difficulties, as David's worthies showed the excellency of their spirits in breaking through a host to gratify their Lord. If the worthies of God in former times had stood upon every difficulty, what would have been done in God's cause? No, this spirit sets upon that which God calls it to. It does what it can, and leaves itself and the issue of its work to God, as Joab in 2 Samuel 10:12: "Let us play the men for our people, and for the cities of our God, and let the Lord do that which seemeth Him good." It was a brave speech that showed an excellent, brave spirit in him.

A poor, low spirit thinks every difficulty an impossibility; but this spirit will not easily entertain thoughts of impossibility in services that are noble and worthy of choice spirits. It will rather think with itself, "Was there never any such thing done before? Or was there never anything that had as much difficulty in it, that was as unlikely as this to come to a good issue, and yet was at last accomplished? Why may not this, then, be done?" So it sets about it without any more objections against it, with this resolution: "That which *has* been done *may* be done."

Such a spirit as this is ashamed to see, hear, and read what great things have been done by others, and what poor things it has all this while been employed in. Suetonius reports that Julius Caesar, seeing Alexander's statue, fetched a deep sigh because he, at that age, had done so little. Yea, so far is a true heroic spirit from being discouraged by difficulties that it is raised by difficulties. Thus it is said of a true godly man that he stirs up himself against the hypocrite, that he holds on his way and grows stronger and stronger (Job 17:8–9). When a difficulty, when any opposition or danger comes in God's ways, now it sees an opportunity offered of showing so much the more love to Jesus Christ, so much the more sincerity and power of grace, to bring so much more honor to God and His cause; and in this it rejoices. This was the reason why the apostles and martyrs rejoiced so much in their sufferings for Christ.

When Ignatius felt his flesh and bones begin to be ground between the teeth of wild beasts, he said, "Now I begin to be a Christian." When Alexander saw an apparent great danger near him, his spirit worked in this manner: "Now," said he, "here is a danger fit for the mind of Alexander to encounter withal." When David at first heard of becoming the king's son-in-law he was troubled at it (1 Samuel 18:22). But when he knew what a difficult and hazardous service he was to undertake for it, then, says the text in the 26th verse, it pleased David well to be the king's son-in-law. That would have discouraged others, who would gladly have had the preferment, but it raised the spirit of David, and made him like the offer the better. And surely this was not an ordinary, common spirit; it was the true magnanimity of the spirit of David.

10. It is a solid, serious spirit. Other spirits are cunning, empty, vain, frothy, rash spirits that produce exceedingly great evils in men. Craftiness of spirit makes men almost incapable of any good. Whatever judgment the Lord lays upon me in this world, yet the Lord deliver me from a vain, subtle, frothy, spirit.

How the blessed, glorious truths of God, which are of infinite consequence, pass by such and are never minded! Nothing sticks by them, nothing abides with them that may be useful for their everlasting good; but this spirit is put into serious, solid frame. It examines the ground of actions, compares one thing with another, looks much at the issue of things; and this must be because the fear of the great God and of eternity is fallen upon it (Isaiah 11:2). These are joined together: the spirit of knowledge, wisdom, spirit of counsel and the fear of the Lord. It converses so much with serious things of high, infinite consequence that it must be put in a serious frame.

11. It is an active, lively spirit, serious but not sullen, not heavy or dull; solid but not stupid. In 1 Peter 2:5, the godly are called lively stones; stones, because of their solidness; lively, because of their activeness. God is himself a pure act, and these spirits have some likeness to Him and nearness with Him. The higher things are, the more active—water more than earth, air more than water, fire more than all. These spirits are raised to the highest excellencies of any creature in this world. They are of quick understanding (Isaiah 11:3), and prepared unto every good work (2 Timothy 2:21). The most noble, excellent activeness is from life, and the more noble and excellent the life, the more noble and excellent the activeness; as sense more than the plants, and the rational life more than the sense, and grace more than that, and glory more than all. The more spiritual, the more active; the more power the form has over the matter, the more active the thing is; and the more the form is sunk, as it were, into the matter, there the less activeness, as in the earth, and all heavy bodies. Now where life is, there the form has most power, and the higher the life, the greater the power. Godly spirits, therefore, are not melancholy, for melancholy makes dull; but they are active and lively, though they may be

heavy and sad if put to some employment not suitable to their spirits. But put them upon spiritual employments, and then you shall find them lively and active. When they have to deal with God, when drawing near unto Him in spiritual exercises, then they are full of life. They are fervent in spirit, seizing the Lord, as in Romans 12:11, "boiling in Spirit," so the word signifies, when serving the Lord. "The effectual fervent prayer of the righteous avails much," says James 5:16. "The working prayer," so the word signifies, and such a working that notes the liveliest activity that can be. Birds, whose motion is on high, fly swiftly when they have gotten up but flutter when they are below. So when the spirits of the godly have gotten up on high to God in spiritual exercises, then they move in a lively mode; but when they are busied in inferior things they are oftentimes dull and heavy.

12. The spirits of the godly are faithful spirits, faithful to God and men, such as will certainly stick to, and will be true to, their principles. You may know where to find them if you know their principles, which are sound and good as before. "The righteous is as an everlasting foundation," Proverbs 10:25. You may build upon him; there is an evenness in all his ways, a constancy, a universality of truth and faithfulness, for it proceeds from his holiness. And therefore those mercies of David (Isaiah 55:3), are called the holy, sure things of David (Acts 13:34). God's holiness makes them sure, being once promised.

There may be a particular faithfulness in some things between man and man, where there are but some common gifts, and the spirit is not this choice spirit, but that faithfulness comes not from a holy frame. And therefore there is not a universality in it.

These are the special qualifications of this other spirit. These are the bright, glistening pearls with which a godly soul, the king's daughter, the spouse of Jesus Christ, is beautiful within, and is an enlightened, free, royal, sublime, humble, sanctified, public, heroic, serious, active, faithful spirit. This is another spirit indeed, not the common ordinary spirit.

*Sixth, another spirit.* It feeds upon other comforts, differing from those that common spirits feed upon. Every life is drawn to the things suitable to the nature of it, and finds some kind of contentment and comfort in the enjoyment of such things. We account life no life unless it has the fillings of it, with things suitable from whence it may have comfort, according to the variety of several principles whereby every creature that has life lives. Such is the variety of comforts in the world. So the life of this spirit must have comforts suitable to it, and because it differs from the life of other spirits the comforts of it are different. It lives upon other comforts. The life of a dog is maintained by carrion, of a swine by swill, of a toad by poison; but what does a man care for these? Though carrion lies in the ditch, though swill is in the kennel, though poison is cast upon the dunghill, he cares not for them; for his life is maintained by, and feeds upon, other comforts. Thus, though the men of the world, living by sense and lust, have no other comforts to feed upon but such as are suitable to them, yet the godly, having a life that has higher and more noble principles, feed upon higher and more noble comforts.

While Nebuchadnezzar lived the life of a beast, he fed on grass; but afterwards, when he was restored to his kingdom and began to live the life of a king, he had other comforts to feed upon and delight himself in. The joys of the spirits of the godly are like the light of the sun, fed by heavenly influence; but the joys of other men are as the light of a candle, fed by base and stinking matter. So Solomon makes the comparison, Proverbs 4:18: "The righteous is as the sun that shines more and more unto the perfect day." And the joys of the wicked he compares to a candle in Proverbs 24:20: "The candle of the wicked shall be put out." The men of the world "have seduced spirits, they feed upon ashes" (Isaiah 44:20). The curse of the serpent is upon them; upon their bellies they go; dust they eat. While they feed upon their swill and husks, the spirits of the saints find bread in their Father's house. Their comforts are inward. A good man is satisfied from himself (Proverbs 14:14). He has a spring within his own breast, he need not shark abroad. "Godliness with contentment is great gain," said the apostle in 1 Timothy 6:6; "godliness with self-sufficiency," so the word signifies.

When Oecolampadius lay sick, his friends asked him whether the light bothered him. He clapped his hand on his breast and said, "Here is light enough." This is spiritual comfort, that which arises from a right frame of spirit. Hence the word in James 5:13 translated "merry" is "the rectitude of the mind," noting that all true mirth must come from the right frame of mind. As for other mirth, I have said that laughter is mad, and I have said to mirth, "What do you do?" When the humors of the body are all in a right temper, there is sweet, sensitive delight in the body. Much more is this true in the spirit when the faculties and the frame of it are in a right temper.

Spiritual comforts that are in things beneath the faculty cannot but be mean, and they debase it. How much beneath the excellency of the spirit of a man is the flesh of beasts, the juice of the grape, any vain sports, or whatever may give content to the sensitive part? But there are comforts that are above the soul—spiritual, heavenly, divine things—and these this spirit feeds upon. They are comforts that the spirit rejoices in before the Lord. That is a sweet and blessed joy, indeed, that is enjoyed before the Lord; and the Lord is most present, most enjoyed. Other vain, sensual spirits have joy, but not before the

Lord. The apprehension of the presence of the Lord dampens all; and therefore they desire not to have mention made of the name of the Lord (Amos 6:10). So to rejoice as to be able to bless God for our joy, so to rejoice as to make the presence of God the chief matter of our joy, this is true joy indeed; this is right spiritual joy. For the spirit to feed upon such comforts is a choice blessing indeed.

They are spiritual comforts, for they are administered to the soul by a special work of the Holy Ghost. It is the office that the Holy Ghost is designed for by the Father and the Son, to be the Comforter, to bring in suitable comforts to the spirits of His servants. And surely the Holy Ghost will not be failing in this work of His. As the Father and the Son have been full and glorious in all their works, so is the Holy Ghost in His. And therefore such must be the comforts of the spirits of God's servants, as must manifest a glorious work of the Holy Ghost in the discharge of what He is sent to do by the Father and the Son. No marvel, then, that the apostle called this joy "unspeakable and glorious." Consider what a difference there must be between the comfort that a little meat and drink and vain sports afford, and the comforts of the Holy Ghost which He conveys into the souls of the godly by the appointment of the Father and the Son! Surely these must be soul-satisfying, soul-ravishing consolations. God is the God of all consolation, and therefore here are all consolations. There is surely infinite good and sweetness, treasures of all excellency in God, and what are they all for but to be comforts for the spirits of His servants to rejoice in! These are not for common, ordinary spirits. They have meat the world knows not of. A stranger shall not meddle in those joys. As men of rank and quality are in higher condition than others, so their comforts and delights are much different from the delights of ordinary people. As God has raised the condition of His people higher than other men, so He has raised their comforts. Children's bread from the Lord's own table is provided for them, while husks and swill serve worldly spirits.

Their comforts are such as are the delights of God Himself and of Jesus Christ. They partake with them in their joys. And surely such joys as they come and join with them in must be sweet and glorious indeed. I and My Father (says Christ) will come and sup with them, and they shall sup with Me. They have dainties that their spirits feed upon that are savory even to the Father and the Lord Jesus Christ. Surely they mistake who think the life of godliness is not a comfortable life, as if the most excellent and highest life should have the worst and lowest condition. Surely it is a gross mistake to think that the spirits of the saints should be the most sad and melancholy spirits! God's Spirit witnesses of them that they are the children of the light, yea, that they *are* light. If they are sad, it is because they meddle too much with things below. It is when their spirits are down. When they get their spirits up to heavenly things, then they can rejoice and sweetly delight themselves. Their hearts are enlarged, their souls are filled with joy.

The birds do not usually sing when they are on the ground, but when up in the air. When on the top of trees, then they sing sweetly. If they are sad and melancholy, it is because they differ no more from the world than they do, because they retain so much likeness to your spirits still in them. Were they freed altogether from the likeness there remains in them to your spirits, they would never be sad more, but their spirits would be filled with everlasting joy. For the present, they rejoice in things suitable to them; and suitableness is the thing that causes comfort in any creature. If the swine could express itself, it would tell you that there is no such comfort as in swill and dung, and wonders that any other creature can take comfort in any other thing like this, because this is the most suitable to their natures. Thus worldly, brutish spirits, because these low, vile things are so suitable to them, think there can be no such comfort in another thing. These things they rejoice in, for they know no better; but if their natures were changed, their greatest comfort would be in despising and vilifying such comforts. St. Augustine, before his conversion, could not tell how he should lack those delights he found so much contentment in. But afterwards, when his nature was changed, when he had another spirit put into him, then he said, "Oh, how sweet is it to be without those former sweet delights!"

You think we have no comforts, or at least not like yours. Know that we can taste natural comforts as well as you, if the poison of sin be not mixed with them. And God gives us leave to rejoice in them. God has made these outward comforts for His servants. Surely God has not made the flowers for the spiders and frogs, but rather for the bee to suck honey out of them. We can taste another manner of sweetness in natural comforts than you can, for we can taste the love of God through them. We can taste them as the comforts that flow from that God in whom all comfort is. We can taste them as forerunners of eternal comforts. A bee can suck honey out of a flower that a fly cannot do.

But, besides these, there are other conveyances of comforts through which our spirits find comforts to feed on; namely, the ordinances where the Lord lets out Himself in a blessed, sweet manner to the souls of His servants. Yet besides, God communicates many comforts immediately. 2 Thessalonians 2:16: "Now our Lord Jesus Christ Himself, and God even our Father, which hath loved us, and hath given us everlasting consolation." Do you think we have no comforts? What, did Jesus Christ come into the world, suffer so many sorrows and miseries, die such a painful death, and all to bring us to a more sorrowful estate than we had before? Let us alone with our comforts; we envy not yours! As Tertullian says in his *Apology Against the Gentiles,* "Wherein do we offend you? If we believe there are other pleasures, if we will not delight in ourselves, it is our own wrong; we reject those things that please you, and you are not delighted with ours."

# CHAPTER TWO

# Wherein the Excellency of This Gracious Spirit Appears

*T*hus they who seek God fully are men of another spirit, and this is their excellency. A spirit thus differentiated from the world where all this is found is an excellent spirit indeed. Here is true worth, all the bravery and glory of the world is not worthy to be mentioned with this. The soul is the excellency of a man, and this is the excellency of the soul. A man's self is his soul. Hence, whereas in Matthew 16:26 it is said, "What shall it profit a man if he gain the whole world, and lose his own soul?" it is said in another evangelist, Luke 9:25, "What shall it profit a man if he gain the world, and lose himself?" Surely, spiritual excellencies are the highest excellencies.

### How spiritual excellencies are the highest excellencies

1. These spiritual excellencies have this property in them: they make a man a better man wherever they are, which bodily excellencies do not for all the riches nor honors in the world. A man is not the better man because he has money, clothes, honors, or a better diet than others. These are but outward things added to him, not intrinsic excellencies.

2. These spiritual excellencies are beginnings of eternal life, the same life we shall have in heaven. Hence the work of God's Spirit in the soul is called "the earnest of the Spirit"; not a pawn but an earnest, for a pawn is to be returned again but an earnest is part of the whole sum that is to follow. That which we have of God's Spirit is part of the glory we shall have fully in heaven. It is not only an evidence unto us that there is glory coming, but it is a beginning of the glory, the fullness whereof is to come afterward. Such a spirit as has this life lives a life far above the common life of the world, even the life of heaven, the same life that angels and saints live in heaven, the life of those blessed spirits there.

We err if we think life in this world compares to the excellent frame of the spirits of God's servants. Life is the chief excellency. There is more distance between the excellency of the meanest, weakest, godly man in the world and the most eminent man for parts and common gifts only than between the meanest and weakest godly soul and the most eminent, glorified saint in the highest heavens. The weakest godly man excels him who is most eminent in common gifts more than the most eminent saint in heaven excels the weakest saint on earth. For the glorified saint is only higher in some degrees in the same excellency, which in the principles, yea, and in some luster, the meanest saint on earth has. He has that which will at last grow up to heaven's glory; but the distance between him and the man who only has the excellencies of parts, learning, or common gifts is essential. All parts and common gifts in the world can never grow up to this.

3. Yea, this is not only the life of angels, the life of heaven, but the life of God Himself; for so it is called by God Himself in Ephesians. Seneca says that reason is part of the divine spirit in man's body. It is much more true of grace; it enables the

soul in some resemblance to come the nearest that can be to live as God lives, to work as God works. It represents God in the highest glory, and therefore it is called "the image of God." This shows more to the world what God is than all the frame of God's creation besides. It is not as an image which has only the dead lineaments drawn, though there is some beauty in this, but as the image in a glass which presents the motion as well as the lineaments; yea, and not only so, but as the son that bears the image of his father, and this represents the life. Or as if a glass had life in it, and so could enjoy the sweetness, the good of that image it represents unto itself. This spirit is such as a living glass of the blessed God, that it enjoys the good and sweetness of that image of God it has in it. Yea, one degree higher, it is called the very divine nature (2 Peter 1:4), as if it were nothing else but a sparkle of the Deity itself.

Seneca has a strong speech concerning man's soul. What can we call the soul (says he) but God abiding in our human bodies? If a soul that has only natural excellencies comes so near God, how near then does it come to Him when raised by those spiritual and supernatural excellencies we have spoken of? Yea, yet there is a higher degree than this. It is called "the glory of the Lord" in Romans 3:23, yea, a higher degree than all the former. The excellency of this spirit is such that it is one spirit with God Himself. See 1 Corinthians 6:17: "He that is joined to the Lord is one Spirit." It was the excellency of Joshua that he had the spirit of Moses upon him; of Elisha that he had the spirit of Elijah; what is it then to have the Spirit of God Himself? Yea, to be one spirit with Him! Put all these then together— godliness by which this other spirit is raised higher than common spirits, it the life of God, the image of God, yea, one spirit with God—and is not here a high and glorious excellency?

4. This makes him, wherever it is, fit to glorify God in the world. And so the soul thus endued is not only a glass to represent a living glass, to enjoy the comfort of what it represents, but as a glass to reflect upon the face of God Himself, the glory of His own image, and that by a principle within itself. Other glasses can reflect upon the thing whose image it has if acted on by a hand externally, but this is by an inward living principle, and so gives God His glory actively, which no other creature can do but angels and men's souls who have these spiritual excellencies in them. Were it not for a few of these spirits, what glory would God have in the world? How little would He be minded or regarded? But these are they who have high thoughts of God, who have trembling frames before Him, who reverence, fear, adore, love, cleave to, trust in, and magnify the name of the great God in the world. These sanctify His name in His worship, they worship Him as a God, and they worship Him in spirit and truth—and such worshippers God seeks (John 4:23). These He highly esteems and greatly rejoices in. These take notice of Him in all His creatures, in the ways of His providence, and use the creatures for Him for whom they are. The glory of God is dear and precious to these. This is the excellency of their spirits: they are not sunk in the dregs of the world, but being kept in some measure in their purity they work up to God, and, as it were, naturally flow to God as to their center.

5. These are such as are fit to stand before the Lord, to converse and enjoy communion with Him. In Daniel 1:4 we read that those who were judged fit to stand in the king's palace before King Nebuchadnezzar must have no blemish. They were to be well-favored and skillful in all wisdom, cunning in knowledge, understanding science, and taught the learning and the tongue of the Chaldeans.

Every spirit is not fit to stand before the King of heaven, to converse with Him. None but the reasonable creature is capable of any such thing as communion with God, and it must be the reasonable creature thus raised. They must be men of other spirits. A man of an excellent spirit cannot endure converse with a base, sordid spirit. Much less can God who is that blessed, holy Spirit.

No creature can have communion with another but such as live the same life. Hence the beast cannot have communion with man because man's proper life is rational. These are the spirits who, being partakers of the life of God, are fitted for converse and communion with Him. Likeness is the ground of all liking in communion; it is the likeness they have to God that makes God delight in communion with them. God loves to dwell with these, and in a special manner. 2 Corinthians 6:16: "As God hath said, I will dwell in them, and walk in them. I will be their God, and they shall be My people." The words are very significant in the original: "I will dwell in them," so the words are. There are two "in's" in the original, as if God could never have near enough communion with them. Psalm 41:12: "He sets them before His face forever," as loving to look upon them. Now how great, how inconceivable a dignity is this, for the poor creature to have this near communion with God!

"Cursed be that man," says that noble Marquis, Marcus Galeaceus, "that prizes all the gold and silver in the world worth one day's enjoyment of communion with Jesus Christ!" He was a man of another spirit, who spoke from his own experience of that sweet communion he had found with Christ, and who had parted with much honor and riches for Him. Enoch and Noah, who were men of other spirits in their generations, are said to walk with God. God took them up even in this world to walk with Him.

Many a sweet turn these spirits have with their God. God delights to have them near Him that He might reveal and communicate Himself to them. These know much of God's mind. The secrets of the Lord are with them, and to them He reveals His covenant. God does not love to hide His face from these. That hidden wisdom which the princes of the world knew not, which "eye hath not seen, nor ear heard, neither hath entered into the hearts of men to conceive," yet has the Lord revealed them to us by His Spirit, said the apostle in 1 Corinthians 2:10, even by that spirit that searches the deep things of God. And by virtue of this communion, these can prevail much with God. It is said of Jacob (Genesis 32:28) that as a prince he had power with God and prevailed. Saint Bernard, in his meditations, gave diverse rules of strictness, of purging the heart, and of being humble and holy. "And when you are thus," said he, "then remember me," knowing the prayers of such a one would much prevail with God for blessing.

6. This spirit is fit for any service, any employment God calls it to. It is a vessel of mercy fitted for the Master's use. Many honorable services God has to be done in the world. Men of ordinary, common spirits are not fit for them. If they would be set about them, they would spoil the work and dishonor God in it. If a man has a choice piece of work, he will not employ one who has no ability to reach to it. He knows the work would fail and it would be his disgrace. When God would employ some about building His tabernacle, He fills them first with His Spirit. So He said of Bezalel and Aholiab. If a man is employed in government, he must be "a man in whom the spirit of God is," as Pharaoh said concerning Joseph (Genesis 41:38). When God chose Saul for government, He gave him another spirit so that he was another man. When God had a piece of work to do of high esteem beyond Saul's reach, He looked for another who

had a more excellent spirit than Saul, and said, "I have found a man according to Mine own heart, who shall fulfill all My will."

The excellency of a thing is in the use of it. What can it do? The excellency of the angels is that they are ministering spirits. The excellency of man is to be serviceable. His excellency is not that he can eat, drink and sport, and go about in finery, but that he is of use, fitted for what service God has to do in the world, that he can further God's ends in his works, that God may say of him, "I have found a man according to Mine own heart who is prepared to fulfill all My will." When Isaiah had his spirit purged in Isaiah 6, signified by that sign of one of the cherubim touching his tongue with a coal from the altar, he presently showed the excellency of his spirit in that, when God had a choice piece of work to do, and asked whom He should send, the prophet readily and cheerfully answered, "Lord, here am I, send me." Do but set the truth of God before these and it is enough. Their spirits, being gracious, close with it, yield to it, obey it, and set about the work they should do. But when men's spirits are corrupt and unsavory, there is such a stir to convince them of God's mind in that which is not agreeable to them, so much ado to prevail with them to the practice, though convinced, that it would grieve a man to have to deal with them.

The excellency of the spirits of God's people is set out to us very sweetly in the expression of the Psalmist in Psalm 18:44: "As soon as they hear, they shall obey Me." There is a willingness of spirit to their work. What God would have, whatever it is, if they apprehend it to be above their reach they cast not off their work but seek God for a supply of ability, knowing that there is spirit enough in God; that God has ways enough to enable the spirits of His servants unto, and carry them on in, any work He sets them about. They know that God will never put any man upon any services but, by one means or another, He will fit His spirit for them. For it is the great delight of God to have men in service to be of spirit fitted for service. When the devil himself has any work to do, he chooses men who have spirits fitted for his work, and in them he delights. If the work requires boldness and impudence, he has men of daring spirits who will set upon it and go through with it. If it requires subtlety, he chooses men of more moderate spirits, who can keep in their passions and secretly and insensibly work their own ends. We read in Revelation 12 that the devil opposes God's saints in fiery and open violence like a dragon; but afterward, in chapter 13, he gives his power to the beast who had seven heads, who would work with more subtlety to draw the world after him.

And we read in Hosea 7:4–7 that those who labored to set up the calves in Dan and Bethel were as hot as an oven in their purpose, intentions, and desires; but because they saw the best way to have the work succeed was not to carry it on at first by open violence, therefore they were content to stay. The baker ceases from raising, after he has kneaded the dough, until it is leavened; and once it is leavened, he puts it into the oven. So they were content to forbear a while, until they had sent fit instruments abroad among the people to leaven them, to prepare them by persuading them that if such a thing were done, it was no great matter. They should still worship the true God. The difference was but the circumstance of the place. And thus, when they were leavened, then they were fit for the oven, that is, for the purpose and intentions of those who desired to set up the calves, which were as hot as an oven. According to any service the devil has for men, he has devices to raise their spirits to that height of wickedness as shall fit them for it.

We have a notable story related of Hospinian concerning this. When the Jesuits had made choice of an instrument for that king-killing service they intended to set him about, they did not put him upon it until they had first raised and fitted his spirit for the service by these means:

First, they brought him to a very private place, in a chapel or oratory, where the knife laid wrapped up in a cloth with an ivory sheath with diverse characters, and "Agnus Dei" written upon it. They drew the knife and wet it with holy water, and hung on the shaft of it some beads consecrated with this indulgence, that as many blows as he gave in killing the king, so many souls he would save out of purgatory. Then they gave the knife to him, commending it in these words: "O thou chosen son of God, take to thee the sword of Jephthah, Samson, David, Gideon, Judith of Maccabeus, of Julius the second who defended himself from the princes by his sword. Go and be wisely courageous, and God strengthen thy hand." Then they fell upon their knees with this prayer: "Be present, O ye cherubims and seraphims; be present, ye thrones, powers, and holy angels. Fill this holy vessel with glory; give him the crown of all the holy martyrs. He is no longer ours, but your companion. And thou, O God, strengthen his arm that he may do Thy will. Give him the helmet and wings to fly from his enemies. Give him Thy comforting beams which may bring joy to him in the midst of all his sorrows." Then they brought him to the altar where the picture of Jacobus Clemens is who killed Henry the third of France, showing the angels protecting him. And then they showed him a crown of glory and said, "Lord, respect this Thy arm, and executioner of Thy justice." Then four Jesuits were appointed privately to speak with him. They told him that they saw a divine luster in his face that moved them to fall down and kiss his feet. And they told him that now he was no longer a mortal man. They envied his happiness, everyone sighing and saying, "Would to God I were in your place, that I might escape purgatory and go immediately into paradise." But if they perceived him to shrink and be troubled after all this, they would sometimes frighten him with terrible apparitions in the night, and sometimes have the Virgin Mary and the angels appear before him.

Thus you see how the devil will have men's spirits fitted for their work; and when they are fit, then he uses them and not before. Much more will God look to have the spirits of His servants fit for their employments, and then only He delights to use them. And those are the spirits who are highly accounted of, who are exceedingly honorable in the sight of God, who are fitted for His own service.

7. This puts a luster of majesty and beauty upon a man. Wisdom (much more all the excellencies of this spirit) makes a man's face to shine. As the light of a lantern puts a luster upon the lantern, so the brightness of these spirits puts a luster upon the men in whom they are. Men of such spirits as these are have a daunting presence in the eyes of those who behold them. It is reported of Basil that such was the majesty and luster of his spirit, appearing in his very countenance, that when the Emperor Valens came unto him while he was in holy exercises, it struck such a terror into the Emperor that he reeled and would have fallen had he not been upheld by those who were with him. When the officers came to take Christ, He only said, "I am He," and let out a beam of the majesty of His deity so that it struck such a fear in them as made them all fall backward. This spirit has a beam of this majesty, and something of the daunting power of it. How unable are wicked men to converse with men of such spirits? They often go from their company convinced, self-condemned; their consciences troubled, and their hearts daunted in them.

8. This spirit makes men fit for any condition that God shall put them into. They know how to yield to God, to find out

God's meaning, to carry themselves in every condition so as to work out that which God would have by it, which men of ordinary spirits cannot do. St. Paul was a man of a most admirable sweet spirit, and he showed it much in this: "I know how to want and how to abound; how to be full and how to be empty." He could go through good report and evil report, and keep his way still and carry his work before him. It is the weakness and vanity of our spirits that makes us think that if we were in such and such a condition, then we could do thus or thus. This is a temptation to hinder us from the duties of the present condition by putting our thoughts upon another. It is the excellency of one's spirit, if the present condition is not suitable to the mind, to make the mind suitable to the condition, that the present duty which God calls us to may go on.

When a joint in the body is set right, it enables it not only to move one way without pain but to move any way according to the use of the member. So where one's spirit is set right, it not only enables it to go on with some comfort in one's condition, but in any condition that God calls us unto, to carry on the work of that condition with joy. And hence the recovering of the spirit from a distempered condition to a right frame is compared to the setting of a member in joint. Galatians 6:1: "If a man be overtaken in a fault, ye which are spiritual, restore such a one in the spirit of meekness." The word signifies, "Put him into joint again." And here you have had the recovery, as of what this other spirit is, so wherein the excellency of this other spirit lies. Now, then, let us make application of all.

# A Discovery to the Men of the World, Whereby They May See that Their Spirits Are Not Like the Spirits of Godly Men

ence, let the men of the world see there is a great difference between their spirits and the spirits of the godly. There are men indeed of excellent spirits. God has such in the world in whom He delights, with whom He converses, whom He employs in high and excellent services. But you are of base, sordid, unclean spirits. The spirit of whoredom, of lying, stubbornness, vanity, and folly is in you. Your spirits are drossy, sensual, froward, malicious, profane, cunning, empty, unsavory, unfaithful, and perverse. What delight can the Lord, who is an infinite, holy, glorious Spirit, take in such? How far are these from any communion with God? It is no marvel that nothing of God, nor any spiritual thing, is savory to them. Oh, the corrupt principles that men's spirits are possessed with, the corrupt rules they go by, and corrupt ends they have in what they do! The base employments they put their spirits to, the noisome distempers of them, and base comforts they feed upon! "The heart of the wicked is little worth," says Proverbs 10:20. Perhaps your lands, your houses may be worth something, but what are your hearts worth? They are worth nothing, full of chaff and dross. They are like children's pockets, full of stones and dirt, while the spirits of the godly are storehouses of the most choice and precious treasures.

When grace is gone from the soul, the excellency is departed from it, as it was said of Ruben that his excellency was departed in respect of that sin of his. How many men or women have fair, comely bodies, a good complexion, and are beautifully dressed up, but within their spirits are most ugly and horrid, full of filth, full of venom and loathsome distempers? Their spirits are full of wounds and putrefied sores, breeding filthiness continually, nothing else but filth and corruption issuing out of them. They are men of corrupt minds, as the apostle says. How unsavory to any who have the least of God in them! If the Lord should give men a view of the horrid deformity and filthiness of their spirits, it would amaze them and sink their hearts in woeful horror. They could not but abhor themselves as loathsome creatures, fit to be cast out from the Lord as an everlasting curse, especially if together with the filth of their own spirits they had a sight of the infinite brightness and glory of the holiness of God, who is an infinite, pure, glorious Spirit. God abhors no other filthiness but the filth of spirits. The devils are abhorred by God because they are unclean spirits. There is no other object of God's hatred but the corruption of spirits.

God made man's soul, at first, a most excellent creature, the very glass of His own infinite wisdom and holiness. But now, what an ugly, base, loathsome creature is it where it is not renewed! If men's bodies were deformed, and ran with loathsome issues and putrefied sores, how dejected would they be in their own thoughts! But certainly this spirit defilement is incomparably worse. If men's bodies were so putrefied that they bred vermin continually (as it is reported of Maximinus), how grievous would it be to them? Their spirits have these loathsome diseases upon them by which they are infinitely more miserable. If they had such a distemper of body that their excrements came from them when they knew not of it, this would be accounted a grievous evil. But their spirits are so corrupt that much filth comes from them and they know not of it. Many are so deeply putrefied in their spirits that they usually swear and speak filthily and know not of it. And they think it is a sufficient excuse that they did not think of it.

It is a rule in nature that the corruption of the best thing is always the worst. A stain in fine linen is worse than in a coarse cloth. So by how much the spirit of a man is more excellent naturally than the body, which is the brutish part, by so much the corruption of the spirit is a greater evil than any the body is capable of. The reason why the devils are so vile and miserable now is that sin seized upon natures that by creation were most excellent. When diseases seize on the natural spirits in the body, they are the most dangerous and deadly. Soul diseases, of all diseases, are the greatest evils and usually prove deadly. Yea, the least spirit-corruption would most certainly prove deadly were it not for the application of that blood that is more precious than ten thousand worlds. Spirit-defilement is such a defilement as defiles everything you meddle with. Titus 1:15: "To the impure all things are impure." Of what use are men whose spirits are so vile? Many make no other use of their spirits but to be, as the philosopher said, of the sensitive soul of the swine. It served for no other use but to be as salt to keep the flesh from stinking. How are many men's spirits employed about nothing else but to make provision for the flesh, and the filthy lusts of it? Oh, that an immortal spirit capable of eternal communion with the blessed God, and of being employed in such high and heavenly exercises as for which it was made, should now come to be so degenerated and debased! Especially, how vile is it that men who, with regard to estates and place, are raised above others, and are trusted with large and blessed opportunities of worthy services for God and the Church, mind nothing but satisfying their lusts, to have their sports. Let the cause of God, Church, or Commonwealth lie bleeding, they regard it not. What a lamentable thing is it to have the weight of great businesses of consequence depending upon such weak-spirited men who mind nothing but vanity and baseness! They have no worthy enterprise in their thoughts. Their spirits are so effeminate that they will do or suffer anything to satisfy their lusts.

There are others who have remaining in them many excellent parts, precious natural endowments, but of what use are they but to enlarge their spirits to be capable of more wickedness than the spirits of other men are—wise to do evil, the fittest instruments for Satan's depths? Who were such enemies to Christ as the scribes and Pharisees, men of the strongest parts? Who were such enemies to St. Paul when he came to Athens as the philosophers there? And no church was founded at Athens, which was the place of the greatest learning in the world. And thus it has been in other succeeding ages.

# CHAPTER FOUR

# The Reason Why the Men of the World and the Godly Can Never Agree

*H*ence we see the reason why the men of the world and the godly can never agree. They are men of another spirit. Where there is a difference of spirits, there can be no agreement. Water and oil cannot mingle. There is no agreement between light and darkness. They look at them as men whose lives are after another fashion. That apocryphal author in the book of Wisdom has an excellent expression to this purpose. In 2:12 he brings in wicked men saying of the godly, "He is clean contrary to our doings, he is grievous unto us to behold; his life is not like other men's, his ways are of another fashion; we are esteemed of him as counterfeits; he abstaineth from our ways, as from filthiness; he commendeth greatly the latter end of the just." Verse 19: "Let us examine him with rebukes and torments." Let the relation and engagements be what they will, yet as long as they are different spirits, they cannot close. What a different spirit was there between Jacob and Esau, who lay in the same womb at the same time! There is outward peace for a while between God's people and some wicked men, but inward closing of spirit there can never be. "The Spirit is in you which the world cannot receive," says our Savior (John 14:17). Antipathies are irreconcilable; no arguments, no means ever used can cause an accord unless there is a change in nature. Nothing in the world puts men's spirits in such a defiant state as grace when it comes. And therefore where the most eminent grace is, there is the greatest disagreement between them and wicked men. How many wicked men cannot but be convinced, regarding some godly men who live with them, that they are better than themselves, that they are conscientious men whose principles are truly godly, and that they walk close to them? The wicked are not able to charge the godly with an ill carriage towards them. The godly seek to do the wicked all the good they can, and yet their spirits cannot close. But as they were wont to say in former times, "Caius Seius was a good man, but he was a Christian," so now such are good men, but they are too strict; and this is enough to keep a perpetual breach between them.

# CHAPTER FIVE

# Learn to Have a Right Esteem of Such Precious-Spirited Men

*I*f the godly are of such excellent spirits, then we should learn to have a right esteem of them. They surely are worthy of precious account, of most honorable esteem, who are men of such excellent spirits, let them be what they will with regard to their outward condition, though never so mean and poor. It does not matter what the ring is made of if the pearl in it is precious. Many very precious spirits have very mean outsides. The Tabernacle was gilded gold within, but the outside was covered with badgers' skins. If the treasure is rich, so what if the vessel is earthen? Surely, these are the excellencies of the earth, the very light and beauty of the world, the glory of God's creation. They give a luster to the places where they live, to the families in which they are; especially if they walk close and faithfully with God indeed, manifesting the excellency of their spirits in their ways. So when they are taken away, the very places where they lived are darkened.

This other spirit of the godly makes a Job scraping his sores on the dunghill, and a Jeremiah sticking in the miry dungeon, more glorious than kings and princes sitting crowned upon their thrones. These are glorious within. God is a Spirit, and He looks on men to see what they are in their spirits and esteems them accordingly. And so should we. What, does brave clothing, does money, do titles of honor raise our dignity? What? Are these the excellency of man's nature? No, certainly! The excellency of man must be that which makes the most excellent and noble part truly excellent, which is the spirit of a man. If a man would know the excellency of anything, as of a sword or any other instrument, he judges it not by the hilt or the inferior part but by what excellency the principal part has. There is a spirit in man, and the inspiration is from the Almighty, a spirit inspired by the Almighty and beautified with His heavenly graces. This ennobles a man indeed. It is the ornament of the hidden man of the heart, the glorious clothing of that which makes truly beautiful and glorious. How did many of the heathen highly prize those in whom they saw any natural excellency of spirit differing from other men! Those among the Romans who were called the "Curii" and "Fabritii" lived very poorly and meanly; yet, being perceived to have more excellent spirits then other men, they were taken from their dinner of turnips and watercress to lead the Roman army. How much more should we honor men in whom we may see divine spirits, the luster of heavenly graces shining in them?

But let us show more particularly that godly men are to be highly prized with regard to this other spirit; as they have received a spirit differing from other men, so they are to have esteem and honor differing from other men. They are not to be looked at as common men, for:

First, this difference of their spirits from other men is a certain sign of the eternal love of God unto them. It comes from the treasure of God's everlasting love, of that choice special love of God from the bowels of God's deepest mercies. It is a most infallible argument that God has set His heart upon them for good. As for other favors, a man may have them more than other men, yet they are not such but may stand with God's hatred and His eternal wrath. And this is a great difference between spiritual mercies and outward mercies, which sets an exceedingly high price upon spiritual mercies above all others. These are the distinguishing mercies, which others are not.

But, second, the spirit receiving these spiritual excellencies from God's choice, everlasting love receives likewise all other mercies from the same fountain. Though in their own nature they are common mercies, yet where this other spirit is present they are received from another fountain than other men receive them, which adds much sweetness and excellency to the mercies we have. They come as fruits of the common bounty and general goodness of God to ordinary men. But to men thus differentiated from others, they come out of the spring of the rich treasures of God's grace, tending to the furtherance of eternal mercies.

Third, the Lord has a special eye upon and delights to dwell with these who are of choice and excellent spirits. "He will dwell with the contrite heart, to revive the spirit of the humble" (Isaiah 57:15). He has a special care for these spirits that they do not fail before Him. He puts His hand under them to support, comfort, and revive them. When we beat ordinary spices, we heed not so much every grain of dust, but some flies out and falls on the ground. But if some special choice costly spice is beaten, then there is care had of every grain of dust so that the least is not lost. So, though God may afflict the choicest spirits of His servants, yet He is very careful that their spirits fail not before Him. As for other common ordinary spirits, He cares not much to let them fail and sink in their affliction, but this is the merciful care of God over those spirits whom He highly esteems.

Fourth, the excellencies of this spirit are eternal excellencies.

They shall abide forever, not vanish, not be taken away as common gifts and other mercies shall. Ezekiel 46:17: "If a prince gives of his inheritance to one of his servants, it is to be his but for a time, and to return unto the prince again; but his inheritance shall be to his sons, for them forever." So when God gives anything to common men, who are but His servants at best, it must return again. God will call for all His mercies from them again; but these soul-mercies of His children shall be their inheritance forever. Hence God calls His church "an eternal excellency" (Isaiah 60:15).

But, fifth, and principally, these spirits are most honorable creatures indeed because they are reserved for other mercies. God gives common mercies to common spirits, but He reserves His choice mercies for choice spirits. "With the pure, Thou wilt show Thyself pure," said David in 2 Samuel 22:27. The words are, "with the choice Thou wilt show Thyself choice." Abraham gave Ishmael and Hagar a bottle of water and a few raisins, and sent them away. But the inheritance was reserved for Isaac. So God gives to other men a few ordinary mercies, but His glorious mercies He reserves for these peculiar ones. And, as it is said of Jehoshaphat in 2 Chronicles 21:3, he gave his other sons great gifts of silver and gold, precious things, fenced cities, but the kingdom he gave to Jehoram because he was the firstborn. So God gives these outward mercies to other men, but the mercies of His Kingdom are reserved for these men of choice spirits who are the firstborn, the chief and most excellent of all God's creatures in this world. "Now we are the sons of God," said St. John, "but it appears not what we shall be." There is more to come hereafter. They do not have spirits that will be satisfied with the things of this world, and therefore are not as ordinary men who have their portion in the things of this world. God delights to fill the capacities of all His creatures with suitable good.

Now these other spirits, by that choice excellency of them, are made capable of far higher mercies than the world can afford. They must be the good things of another world that can fill them, and those are reserved for them. The bodies of the saints, because they are joined to such precious souls, shall be like the glory of the sun, yea, shall excel in glory. How glorious, then, shall their souls be for whose sake their bodies shall be thus glorious! We look upon great heirs who have great inheritances to come with high esteem, though they have little for the present. These are the great heirs of heaven, co-heirs with Jesus Christ Himself. These they are who are delivered from the wrath to come and are to be made partakers of the glory that is to be revealed. The Lord gives them no great matters in comparison now, because He has reserved so much for them afterwards. As nature is not very exquisite in her work in inferior things where she intends some higher excellency, so the God of nature, intending such high and glorious things hereafter for His saints, does not so much regard to give them these inferior things for the present.

QUESTION. But what are those reserved mercies you speak of that God has for these?

ANSWER. Not intending a treatise on that glory that God has for His choice ones, I will only give you these five general things:

First, these mercies are prepared mercies, prepared before the foundations of the world were laid, and again prepared by Jesus Christ, who is gone before to heaven to that end, as He tells us Himself, to prepare mansions for us in John 14:2. Now this is spoken after the manner of men, who do not usually make long and great preparations but for some great work in hand. Surely, these mercies must be great which God in His wisdom power, and mercy has been preparing from all eternity.

Second, they are other mercies than Adam, than mankind should have had, than they could have attained unto. If he had stood in his innocence, man indeed should then have been forever happy, but not according to that height of happiness and glory that now are provided for those who are the beloved of the Lord.

Third, these reserved mercies are such as must set out God's magnanimity, that God may show to angels and all His creatures what His infinite wisdom, power, and goodness can do for poor creatures to raise their conditions to a height of glory. Surely that glory must be high that is raised to that end. If a king should do anything of purpose to show his magnificence, it must be some great thing. It is not a common, ordinary thing that can set forth the magnificence of a king, much less that can set forth the magnificence of the great God. When Ahasuerus would make a feast and Nebuchadnezzar would build a palace to show to their people their greatness, they were great things. So surely here, that which must show the greatness of the great God must be great indeed.

Fourth, these mercies must be such as may show to angels and all the world how infinitely well-pleased God the Father is with the obedience of His Son in giving Himself up to death for the purchase of mercy. Surely that mercy thus purchased must be great. If there had been no higher good for man but to eat, drink, and have pleasure in the flesh, certainly Christ would never have died to purchase this. But there were higher things than these that Christ looked at. These are but poor things for God to show by them how infinitely He is well-pleased with the obedience of His Son to the death. That which must demonstrate this cannot but be very great whatever it is, and that, yea, the fullness of that, is the mercy reserved for these choice ones.

Fifth, these are other mercies (in some respect higher) than the very blessed angels themselves have, and that because:

1. Man's nature is more highly advanced than theirs, being hypostatically united to the divine nature.

2. The righteousness whereby the saints come to glory is a higher righteousness, a more excellent righteousness than that of the angels. Though theirs is perfect in its kind, theirs is the righteousness but of mere creatures. But the righteousness of the saints is the righteousness of He who is both God and man.

3. The sonship of the saints is founded in a higher right than that of the angels, namely in the Sonship of the second Person in the Trinity.

4. They are the members of Jesus Christ, and so in a nearer union with Him than any other creature.

5. They are the spouse of the Lamb, whereas the angels are but ministering spirits as the servants of the Bridegroom, but the saints are the bride.

Surely, then, the mercies reserved for these choice spirits are choice and glorious, not only other mercies than others have, or they themselves have now, but other mercies than they are able to imagine. These who have received such mercy are to be looked upon as most blessed and honorable creatures.

# A Rebuke to Those in this Vile World Who Have Vile Conceits of this Spirit, and Abuse Men of Such Excellent Spirits

*I*f the spirits of godly men are this precious, how vile then is this base world which has such irrational, absurd conceits of this spirit, and which so scorns and abuses men of such excellent spirits!

There are two branches of this use. In the first, the vile conceits that men of this world have of this spirit are rebuked, for:

1. They think godliness makes men fools.

2. They think it makes them cowards, to be men of no mettle and valor, poor-spirited men.

3. They think this spirit to be a turbulent spirit. As Ahab said of Elijah in 1 Kings 18:17: "Art thou he that troubles Israel?" Luther was called the trumpet of rebellion.

4. And last, they think them to be factious spirits.

BRANCH 1. For the first of these, what is more ordinary than to cast this aspersion upon godliness, that it makes men to be dull, heavy, stupid fools, not fit for the great and high things of the world. And therefore they labor to stifle any beginnings of godliness in their children, or anyone near to them, for fear it should hinder their parts and take away the quickness of their wits and bravery of their spirits. Unless you think that to be the only bravery of spirit, to venture upon anything that may further your own ends; not to fear sin, nor the displeasure of an infinite God; to let out your hearts to the utmost in satisfying your own desires; to examine nothing by rule but to do whatever is good in your own eyes; to rejoice in the ways of sin and to deceive yourself in the proud swellings of your own heart; to be able to scorn at conscience, humiliation for sin, and strictness in God's ways as too mean a thing for men of such quality, of such birth as you are, of such estates, hopes, preferments, and designs as you have, things fitter for poor snakes, meaner people, contemptible silly souls to look after—if this is the excellency of your spirits, then godliness refutes them indeed. Yea, it debases them as low as hell itself. It casts shame in the faces of, and breaks in pieces, such haughty, swollen spirits as these are. It brings them down to lie at God's feet as poor, contemptible creatures in their own eyes, loathing and abhorring themselves, as there is infinite cause they should, and judging themselves worthy to be destroyed.

But as for any true natural excellency of spirit, godliness does not quench it, but raises it, beautifies it, and perfects it. It is either gross ignorance or desperate malice that causes these spirits in men; yea, there is much blasphemy in them. What? Shall the work of God's grace, wherein the glory of God consists, which is the life of God, the image of God, the divine nature, as has been shown, shall it be the debating, the besetting, the duping of men's spirits? What, does the holiness that makes God glorious make man contemptible and vile? Does that which makes God so honorable in the eyes of the blessed angels and saints make man a sot and a fool in the eyes of men? Oh, that ever there should be such malice in the hearts of men against the grace of God, ever to have such vile conceits of it! Pray, if it is possible, that this thought of your heart may be forgiven you. If malice did not blind men, they might see that the Lord has had, and still has, some of His saints as eminent in any outward true excellence as any in the world. There are as great scholars, as brave courtiers, as any living; as deep in policy, as profound in learning, as complete every way as any whatsoever.

Who was more eminent in learning than Moses, who was learned in all the learning of the Egyptians? Who ever had a higher strain of eloquence than Isaiah? Who ever was more profound than St. Paul? And in latter times, yea, even in our days, the church has not lacked worthy and glorious lights who have been exceedingly eminent in all that natural excellency could make them, even their enemies being judges. What braver courtiers ever lived than Joseph, Nehemiah, and Daniel? Could godliness, in the power and life of it, in the strictness of it, stand with bravery of spirit and natural excellencies then? And can it not do so now? God often chooses the poor in the world to be rich in faith, the foolish things in the world to confound the wise, and the weak things of the world to confound the strong; and base things and things despised (1 Corinthians 1:26–27). Yet when men are godly, their parts are not debased by their godliness but raised. Many poor, weak men before were of mean, natural abilities, yet put them now upon spiritual things and what strength of parts do they show in prayer, in conference about the mysteries of God, in discerning the subtleties and wiles of Satan, in finding out the corruptions of their own hearts, in wisely ordering their affairs for God and for the furtherance of their own eternal good. They are wise in the right choice of the highest end, and prudent in the right disposing of the best means tending thereunto. These things are not the works of fools, of poor, silly, simple men. They require quickness of understanding and depth of judgment.

There are five reasons why godliness must raise man's parts:

1. Because it purges from many lusts that darken and besot men in their parts.

2. It employs men in conversing with high, spiritual, and heavenly things.

3. It makes men serious, and so strengthens their judgments in the apprehension of things.

4. It makes men make conscience to improve their time in the use of all means and helps they can, to enable and fit themselves for service.

5. It causes men to employ their parts faithfully, and so they come to have the blessing of God upon them, for the increase of them according to His promise, "To him that hath, it shall be given."

Again, godliness does not make men cowards. Surely, it does not hinder spiritual valor. Who ever were greater soldiers, more eminent in true valor and fortitude, than Joshua, David, Gideon, Barak, and others who through faith subdued kingdoms (Hebrews 11:32–33)? That is baseness of spirit and lack of valor that makes a man a slave to sin and the devil. A slave has no heart for any worthy service, to free himself from his station, but lies down under it and carries the fetters and yoke of his bondage about with him wherever he goes. That is cowardly baseness that brings conscience into a servile subjection, that cowardly baseness that will suffer the cause of God to be betrayed rather than venture anything for it. What greater argument is there that men lack true spirit of fortitude than this? Godliness puts a spirit of fortitude into men that will not suffer them to be thus debased. And where appears the like courage in any as in these when they are called to stand for the truth? "Though all the tiles of the houses in the city of Worms were devils, yet there would I go to testify to the truth," said Luther.

Again, it is not a turbulent spirit; for turbulence of spirit makes men cruel and malicious. This spirit causes men to love their enemies, to do all the good they can to them. Turbulent spirits seek only their own ends. They care not what becomes of others. So it is that they may but warm themselves; they care not what house be on fire. They are boisterous in things that concern themselves.

But the saints of God in whom this other spirit rules are meek, gentle, and yielding in their own cause, ready to put up with wrong in all quietness. Take them in things that only concern themselves and you shall find none so readily, so freely, so cheerfully denying themselves as they. And again, turbulent spirits do not love to examine things by rule, to call things to account, but follow their own fiery humor and set upon their own will with violence. But godliness takes men off from this ruggedness and turbulence of spirit and makes them gentle and peaceable. Let them be never so forward, never so zealous in anything, yet if you will call them to examine things by rule, they will meekly and patiently hear you. Yea, a child shall lead them (Isaiah 11:6).

And yet further, turbulent they are not; for none are more obedient to authority than they. None see that majesty of God in authority as they do. None obey authority out of conscience as they do. If the will of men in authority, rather than genuine authority itself, shall require anything that the authority of heaven forbids, they do not do that because they cannot obey for conscience's sake. But so sacred do they account authority that they would have no obedience performed to it but obedience for conscience's sake. Blind obedience the church of God has long ago exploded as too servile for Christian spirits. This would be more servile than selling men's bodies in the market as slaves, which Christianity abhors. It would be too uncharitable a conceit of Christian magistrates to think that they should require of any person, or expect from any, other obedience than in and for the Lord. And in this obedience, those who are godly are so forward as they are judged turbulent for being overly forward to maintain the honor of authority, as some think, when, according to their places, they promote the execution of laws made by authority, and that of those laws which are of the highest consequence for the furtherance of piety and peace.

Again, factious spirits they are not because they seek above all things to keep to the maintenance of, and obedience to, the primitive truth. That is faction that sides against that. Tertullian had a notable expression in his *Apology for the Christians against the Gentiles,* to clear God's people of the charge of being men of factious spirits. It seems that aspersion was cast upon them then, which was about 1,400 years ago. His expression was this: "When good men, when honest men, meet together, when godly men are gathered together, it is not to be called a faction but a court; and on the contrary, the name of faction is to be applied to them who conspire to the hatred of good and honest men."

BRANCH 2. Now the second follows, which is the rebuking of the men of the world for the ill use they give to men who are of such excellent spirits. The excellencies of the spirits of the godly challenge all the good use that can be, but it is little they meet with. They are, for the most part, abused by the men of this vile world as if they were the vilest scum and filth of the earth; yea, so indeed they account them. So said St. Paul in

1 Corinthians 4:13: "We are made as the filth of the world and are the off-scouring of all things unto his day." Why? What was St. Paul, and what were those who were with him, who were so accounted? Were they not men of most excellent and admirable spirits? St. Paul was one of the most excellent-spirited men who ever lived upon the earth, and did as much service for God as ever any mere man did since the beginning of the world. And yet how vilely was he thought of! How contemptibly was he used! Was he not put into stocks and whipped? Did he not lack clothes and victuals? And as for the others who were with St. Paul, they were men of whom the Holy Ghost gives this witness, that they were the very glory of Jesus Christ (2 Corinthians 8:23). O unworthy world, that ever should have such men live among them! Those who are the delight of angels, yea, of God Himself, how are they abused in this wicked world as if they were dogs or the basest scum and filth of the earth! What scorn and contempt are cast upon them! The most abject of men think themselves good enough to reproach and abuse them. Would it not be a grievous sight to see some base laborer have power over the body of some noble prince, to abuse it by stripes or any other contumelious, sordid manner? But a more grievous thing it is to see the vile and base spirits of the world, who are nothing but sinks of filth themselves, abuse men of such noble and excellent spirits as if they were more vile than dirt.

It was the bitter complaint of Jeremiah in Lamentations 4:2 that the precious sons of Zion, comparable to fine gold, were esteemed as earthen pitchers. They are such as blessed spirits would honor, if they were with them, yet here they are cast out as filth. What grief is sufficient to lament the sight of such filthy swine trampling under their feet such precious pearls! Yet in all ages thus it has been. Those were indeed the truly honorable upon the earth, such precious and excellent-spirited men of whom the world was not worthy, and yet they have been most vilely abused, and are so still by this wretched world who knows not wherein true worth and excellency consist. In Matthew 5:12 Christ told His disciples how ill the world would use them. He told them they have as good use from it as the prophets had before them. How was Micaiah (a man of very sweet and excellent spirit) contumeliously used? He was struck on the mouth and shut up in prison to be fed with water and bread, while 430 false prophets, most base-spirited men, were fed delicately at Jezebel's table.

How was Jeremiah used? He was thrown into the dungeon and stuck up almost to the ears in the mire. The Word of the Lord was made a reproach unto him daily. David before them (a man in whom God's soul delighted) complained that he was a reproach of men and despised of the people. All who saw him laughed him to scorn. They shot out the lip and shook their head at him (Psalm 22:6–7). Job before him was made a byword of the people, and as a timbrel unto them, as he said of himself in Job 17:6.

The same use had the blessed apostles, who were filled with the Spirit of God. None were more scorned, persecuted, or condemned than they. The most worthy and famous men in the primitive times found no better use than these. It would be an infinite task to list all of them in particular. Ignatius, Polycarp, Athanasius, Chrysostom, Basil, and the rest were reproached, banished from their people, persecuted, and exceedingly contumeliously used. In later times, the more excellent the spirits of men were, the worse use they ever found from the world. We might instance, for example, Wycliffe, Huss, Luther, Zwingli, Musculus. I cannot pass by that sad example of Musculus who was a man of as brave a spirit as any who lived in his time, a very learned and godly man. Yet after he had labored much in the work of the Lord in his public ministry, he was so ill used of the world that he desired to get into a weaver's house and learn to weave so that by it he might get himself and his family bread. And within a while he was accounted unworthy of *that* preferment and was thrust out of the house by his master the weaver. Then he was forced to go to the common ditch of the town and work with his spade to get his living.

Whose heart does not bleed to hear of these former examples and divers others, men of most precious spirits thus ill used by this unworthy world, even such in whom Christ rejoices that ever He shed His blood for them (Isaiah 53:11)? These are such as He will glory in before His Father and the blessed angels, yet thus are they abused by this wicked world. The more eminently the Spirit of Christ appears in any, the more is the rage of evil men against them. It is reported of tigers that they rage when they smell the fragrance of spices. The fragrance of the graces of God's Spirit in His people, which is delightful to God and His saints, puts wicked men into a rage. Base-spirited men, however, have the world smile on them according to their heart's desire. Oh, the providence of God who suffers such indignities to be offered to His most precious and choice servants! But by this means the excellency of their spirits appears in greater brightness, their graces shine in the clearer luster.

All God's servants have His Spirit in them, but when any of them suffer reproach and ill use at the hands of the world, then the Spirit of God and of glory rests on them. Then the glorious Spirit of God is upon them according to the promise of God unto them (1 Peter 4:14). And their persecutors may in part perceive, even while they are using them ill, that they are men not of common, not of ordinary spirits who are thus ill used by them. They may see in that meekness, that patience, that humility, self-denial, faith, holy carriage, requiting good for evil, praying for their abusers, doing all the good they can to those who use them worst, that constancy, spiritual cheerfulness, sweet contentedness, that holy boldness, humble courage, heavenly magnanimity— they may see such traits and wonder that their conscience should not misgive them even while they are abusing them, that their conscience does not tell them, "Surely these men we mistake in. They are led by other principles than we know of. They have something within that supports them that we understand not." It is a wonder that men are not afraid to abuse them as they do. In Numbers 12:8, the Lord said to Miriam and Aaron concerning Moses, when they spoke against him, "Were ye not afraid to speak against My servant, against Moses?" Were he only My servant, though he were not Moses, should you not be afraid? But when My servant Moses, such an eminent servant of Mine, in whom so much of My Spirit appeared, should you not be even more afraid to speak against him?

Certainly, the Lord will not always suffer precious, choice-spirited men to be trampled under foot. He looks upon them in their lowest estate as His jewels even while they are in the dirt. But time will come when He will make up His jewels (Malachi 3:17), and then there shall be seen a difference between the righteous and the wicked, between him who serves God and him who serves Him not (verse 18). God will own the excellency of the spirits of His servants to be the image of Himself, and what confusion will this be to the ungodly of the world when the Lord, before men and angels, shall own that for the luster and beauty of His own excellency which they, when time was, made matter of their scorn and objects of their hatred! When God shall come to them, as Gideon to Zebah and Zalmmna, Judges 8:18–20, " 'What manner of men were they,' said Gideon to them, 'whom you slew at Tabor?' They answered, 'As thou art, so were they;

each one resembled the children of a king.' Then he said, 'They were my brethren, the sons of my mother; as the Lord liveth, if you had saved them alive, I would not have slain you'; but now he says to Jether, his firstborn, 'up and slay them.' "

So shall God hereafter say to the men of the world, "What were those men, and what did they, whom you so hated and abused? What? Were they some vile-spirited men? How did they carry themselves?"

Your consciences shall be forced then to answer, "O Lord, we must confess, they were those who kept themselves from the common pollutions of the world. They lived strictly in their ways; they walked unblameable in their course; they were very forward in the duties of the worship and service of God."

The Lord shall then answer, "What? These men were My saints. This was My holiness, My image, My glory. These were not common, ordinary men. These were My choice ones, men precious in My eyes, separated from the common sort of the world for My praise. If you had loved them, prized them, and honored them as the choice of the earth, if you had followed their example, I would not have slain you; but now you shall perish everlastingly."

# CHAPTER SEVEN

# It Is No Dishonor to Be Singular. Seven Notes to Discover that Godly Men's Differing from Other Men Proceeds Not from Proud, Humorous Singularity, but from the Choiceness and Excellency of Their Spirits

*I*f godly men are men of another spirit, and this is their commendation; why then should any account it to be a dishonor to be singular from the world? Singularity is cast upon God's servants as their disgrace, but certainly it is their glory. They are singular and their ways are singular, it is true, and they avow it, they rejoice in it, and bless God for it. It is impossible but that it should be so for they are of another spirit, a peculiar people, separated from the world, set apart for God. Their separation is a wonderful separation, Exodus 33:16: "So shall we be separated," says Moses, "I and Thy people, from all the people that are upon the face of the earth." The word is, in the original, "We shall be wonderfully separated." No marvel then, though their singularity be such as the world, who knows not their principles, wonders at it. Their ways are different from other men, aye; that is true indeed, who can think otherwise? Their principles, their estates, their dignities, and their hopes are raised higher than other men's. Would Saul have been offended if his former acquaintance had complained, "Oh, now, Saul, he minds other things, goes on in other ways, lives after another fashion than we do"? Aye, that is true indeed, for his condition is altered; his estate is raised higher than yours. He has another spirit.

To complain that God's servants are singular from others is as if you should complain that pearls are more glistening than dirt and gravel. Their way, their lives, are singular. Why, how would you have them live? Would you have them live according to the common course of the world? They cannot, for they have not received the spirit of the world, but another spirit.

When the Spirit of God would set out the greatest misery of men, that they are the children of wrath, without God in the world, without hope, it is stated that they lived according to the common course of the world (Ephesians 2:2). And these two concepts are joined together: living according to the common course of the world, and according to that spirit that rules in the children of disobedience. As long as they were acted upon by that spirit, they lived so; but now there is another Spirit that they are influenced by, and would you have them live still as they did before? Certainly it cannot be. You complain of dissimulation, and that justly; but what is dissimulation if this is not, where there is not a suitableness between the inward principles, the inward frame and disposition of the spirit, and the outward actions?

Now if God's people should not live singular lives, certainly their outward actions would not be agreeable to the inward principles, frames, and dispositions of their spirits, for they are singular, differing from other men's. As there may be dissembling by which a man seems better than he is, so there may be dissembling by which we seem worse than we are. Is there not as much evil in a life differing from the spirit as in a spirit differing from the life? If a man seems to be godly and is not, it is an argument the man is vile who will thus play the hypocrite. But it is a commendation to godliness that men will account the very seeming of it to be honorable. But if a man has godliness in his heart and yet his life is no other than other men's, this would argue that a man is ashamed of godliness itself. Here godliness itself would suffer. It is as if it were such a dishonorable thing as would bring shame to a man if it appeared; as if though indeed it must be reserved in the heart, for necessity's sake, yet it must be kept down, not suffered to appear in the life, for fear it be a disgrace to men. Is not here then as great an evil, in this way of dissimulation, as in the other? Better all the men of the world had shame cast upon them than that godliness should have the least stain. Surely, then, where the spirits of men are other spirits, singular choice spirits, their lives ought to be, and must be, other lives, singular from other men. Their conscience witnesses to them that their spirits are changed, that they are other than what they were; yea, and it witnesses for them that their lives are other lives, singular from other men. And in this witness their souls rejoice.

But is there not a proud, fantastic singularity? May not pride, sullenness, and fancy carry men on in singular ways, differing from other men, thinking themselves to be wiser than others, loving to satisfy some odd humors of their own? If it were any choiceness or excellency of their spirits, it would be another matter; we would not speak against them. But it is this proud, hypocritical, humorous singularity we speak against.

To this I answer, if you indeed should do as they do, if you should live after a different manner from the common course of the world having no other principles than those you have, it would certainly be singularity, pride, hypocrisy, and humor in you. Your consciences would tell you this, and that because you had no principles to carry you out in this way. You do not have spirits suitable to it; and you, judging others by what you feel in yourselves, come to think that the different ways of God's servants are only from pride and humorous singularity. Yea, and they themselves know that there was time indeed wherein, if they would have done as now they do, it would have been no other in them than what you now accuse them of; namely, when their spirits were as other men's spirits are. But now they know that they have other principles, other qualifications of spirit, than formerly they had. But surely, you do not think indeed that their different lives come from proud and humorous singularity; for if you did, why did your consciences so well approve of them when you lay on your sick beds? When you apprehend yourselves going before the great God, then you could wish it were with you as it is with them.

But what do you say? If you thought it was not from this pride and conceitedness you speak of, then you would think it were well. Then you would join in justifying them, if you were sure it was from a choice, excellent spirit in them.

Well, then, let God's servants rejoice in this, that they know it is not from pride, that it is not from humor, that they run not into excess of riot as others do, but from the work of God upon their spirits. And this witness they have for themselves, this they have to encourage themselves in, that if the men of the world did but know the principles from whence they work, as they know them themselves, even they would justify both these godly ones and their ways.

Further, there is a way of God that is real, that tends to life. Whatever way it is, this is certain—it must be different from the common course of the world. And if this is not it in which God's people walk, tell us what is that way and we will walk in it. The Scriptures tell us that the way to life is narrow and few walk in it, and the other way is broad that tends to death. We cannot therefore but fear when we see the mark of a way that leads to death. Christ's flock is but a little flock. Luke 12:32: "Fear not, little flock." There are two diminutives in the original. The word translated "flock" signifies a little flock, but, that the exceeding littleness of it might appear, Christ adds another word. So the words are, "Fear not, little little flock." St. John, in 1 John 5:19, says, "The whole world lies in wickedness, but we know that we are of God." What a singularity was this in St. John? How does he distinguish a few odd, contemptible people from the whole world? We are of God, and yet the whole world lies in wickedness, and the world surely is not grown better since.

But that you may see that the way of the godly is not from singularity or humor, take these evidences and judge according as conscience shall tell you is truth.

First, where humor and conceited singularity prevail with men, there is no evenness, no constancy in their ways, no proportion of one thing with another in their course. They are singular and humorous in some odd, foolish things, but in other things, where they have as much reason to be singular, they do as others do. But in God's people you shall see an evenness, constancy, and proportion in the course of their lives. That which makes them singular in one thing makes them so in all other things of the same nature. They are not as humorous people who have their fits and take them out of their fits; those are other men who can be as different from themselves as they are from other men. But where the Spirit of God guides, though there is no more difference from other men, yet there is less difference from themselves.

Second, those who do things purely out of singularity, simply to be different from others, care less for such things they do out of that principle, when they come to be common, than they did before. But it is not so here in the ways of godliness. The more common the ways of godliness grow, the happier these people are; the more God's people rejoice and bless themselves in these behaviors, the more lovely and amiable they are in such people's eyes.

Third, humorous, singular men differ exceedingly one from another. One will be singular in one thing and another in another, but God's people go all the same way. They have the same course with such as they never saw. Observe the spirits and ways of godly men in all places of the world. Though their education, their constitution, their employments, and their former principles are exceedingly different, yet now, for the main part, they are the same. They favor and relish the same things; they delight in the same way of holiness, which evidently shows they are led and acted on by one and the same spirit. Though they may differ in some things of lesser moment one from another, yet they differ very little among themselves in things wherein their difference from the world principally lies. In those things for which the world dislikes them and their ways, there is a general agreement in the spirits of all godly men in such things. For example, they agree in fearing the least sin as a greater evil than any outward misery, in loving the strictest ways of holiness; in laboring to keep themselves pure, as much as they can, from the sins of the times and places where they live. In these and such like things, which are most proper to godliness, and for which they are judged singular, there is a general agreement of all the spirits of the godly throughout the world.

Fourth, proud, conceited singularity displays itself especially in things that are noticed by others. If others fail to take notice of them, they quickly grow weary of what they do; and this is the best way to deal with such people, to neglect them. Let them perceive nobody thinks them worthy of regarding, of once minding them, and this makes them weary sooner than all the opposing can ever do. The end of singularity is that it might be observed. This is the humor of these people—they would fain be noticed for something, let it be what it will. Observance is the thing that feeds this humor. Where this is not present, it soon grows weary of itself. And hence, when these people are alone and none can observe them, they do as other men do.

But now the special work of godliness, wherein God's people differ from other men, that in which their souls most delight and are most fully exercised in, is in secret things not subject to the view of the world: "The King's daughter is all glorious within." If there is a little godliness outwardly, there is much more inwardly. Where there is a little wickedness without, there is an abundance in the heart. Godly men are most eminently godly in inward things. The countenance and voice of the Church are most sweet and comely in secret places. Song of Solomon 2:14: "My dove that art in the holes of the rock, in the secret places of the stairs, show me thy sight, let me hear thy voice, for thy voice is sweet and thy sight is comely." Godly men dare not but be godly before men, for so Christ commands them: "Let your light shine before men, that others may see your good works." But it is one thing to do that which may be seen, and another to do it to the end that it may be seen, and to make that the highest end. If they make their end that the light may be seen and not that they may be seen, and that their Father in heaven may be glorified and not themselves glorified, it is no other than Christ would have. But between God and their souls, there is the chief work of godliness. There the souls of God's servants most expiate themselves; there they are most themselves; there is their most proper element. Wherefore, surely, it is not a humor of singularity.

Fifth, if it were humorous singularity, it would not bring them so much sweet peace and heavenly joy when they are upon their sick and deathbeds, when they have to deal with God in a special manner. When they are to appear before the great God to receive the sentence of their eternal doom, when they are to enter upon eternity, how many then bless God that ever He put it into their hearts to go another way, not according to the common course of the world? Though humor and conceitedness may please and give contentment for a while, yet they can never bring such peace and joy in sickness and death, when the soul sees it has to deal with such an infinite, holy God, such a dreadful majesty. None apprehends the glory and majesty of God as the godly do. None understands what eternity means as they do. The sight of these things would shake men out of a humor. It is not humor that can stand before God, when the eternal misery or happiness of the creature is rightly apprehended. It is time now to lay aside humors and conceits; and yet then when these things are most clearly, most powerfully apprehended by God's servants, even then they are more for the ways of God in which they differed from the world than ever they were before. It is now their greatest grief that they have no more differed from them than they have, and if they were to begin again they would differ far more than ever they did.

Sixth, surely it is not humorous, conceited singularity because most men who have enlightened consciences, when they are most serious in their best moods, are of this mind. If you will go by multitudes, we dare venture upon this, yea, we dare challenge upon this argument, only with these two cautions:

The men you bring in must be men of enlightened consciences, for what have we to do with others who are blind and ignorant? Though there may be many thousands of them as never before, they can add nothing at all to the cause.

Let the judgments of men be taken when they are most serious, when they are best able to judge. Do not take them when they are in a passion, when their lusts are up, but when their spirits are calmed and in the best temper, when conscience has the most liberty to speak indeed what it thinks. And of such men, in such times, we shall have the most on our side. Therefore, surely, it is not a humor of singularity that guides them in the way of godliness.

Seventh, it is not singularity, for we have the prophets, apostles, martyrs, and saints of God before us, clouds of witnesses, thousands and thousands of them. And every one of them is worth ten thousands of others. Chrysostom had an expression in one of his sermons to the people of Antioch: "It is better to have one precious stone than to have many half-pennies; so one godly man is better than multitudes of others." And Saint Cyprian had the like expression in one of his epistles: "Do not attend to the number of them, for one that fears God is better than a thousand wicked." It is safe to follow the way of good men, according to Proverbs 2:20: "Walk thou in the ways of good men, and keep the ways of the righteous."

Now then, let neither the ways of godliness or godly men ever be blamed for their singularity. Other spirits must lead into other ways. It was laid to Luther's charge that he was an apostate. He confesses himself to be one, but a blessed and a

holy apostate, one who had fallen off from the devil. So we confess, this is singularity that differentiates God's servants from
this vile wicked world in which they live, whereby they live as
men of anther world, as indeed they are.

# CHAPTER EIGHT

# Bless God for Making This Difference Between Your Spirits and the Vile Spirits of the Men of the World

Seeing this other spirit is so excellent and blessed, then you to whom God has given other spirits, learn to bless God for them. The mercies of God to men's spirits are the greatest mercies. Though your conditions are meaner than others in other respects, yet if your spirits are raised to a higher excellency than others, you have infinite cause to bless the Lord, as did Paul in Ephesians 1:3: "Blessed be the Lord, which hath blessed us with all spiritual blessings in heavenly things, in Christ." What if God has not abounded to you in outward honors, estates and delights? Yet if He has abounded to you in wisdom, holiness, faith, and humility, you have no cause to complain. Where God gives His Spirit, in the gifts and graces of it, there He gives all good things. Hence, whereas Matthew 7:11 says, "How much more shall your Father in heaven give good things to them that ask Him?", Luke 11:13, bringing in Christ speaking upon the same occasion, says, "How much more shall your heavenly Father give the Holy Ghost to them that ask Him?"; as if it was all one to give His Spirit and to give all good things.

Spiritual blessings make all outward crosses light and easy. Proverbs 18:14: "The spirit of a man will sustain his infirmities." Spiritual blessings have this excellency in them, that they cause a man to feel no need of many outward things, which others know not how to go without. And it is as good to be in such an estate, to have no need of a thing, as to enjoy it when we want it. And further, it is the excellency of spiritual blessings to keep down the body and to carry the spirit above the body. It was the excellency and glory of the martyrs that their spirits were so satisfied with mercies they had that they so little regarded their bodies when they suffered grievous torments as if they had not been their own. Thus Sozomen reports of them.

Spiritual blessings are such as enable men to improve all other blessings they enjoy. Without these, the greatest of other blessings would prove to be the greatest curses to us. And yet, further, these blessings upon our spirits cost God infinitely more than other blessings do. Other blessings God can give at a low rate, but these cost the dearest heart-blood of His own Son. And therefore, above all, let God have the praise of these. Outward bodily mercies we are unworthy of, but when we consider these let us say as David in Psalm 66:16: "Come and hearken, all ye that fear God, and I will tell you what He hath done for my soul." There God has magnified His mercies toward me indeed.

You may remember how base your spirits once were, how blind, foolish, drossy, sensual, and, it may be, malicious. This Paul calls to mind, to stir up himself and others to praise God for that blessed change He had wrought in his and their spirits. Titus 3:3–4: "For we ourselves also were in times past," said he, "unwise, disobedient, deceived, serving divers lusts, living in maliciousness and envy, hateful, and hating one another; but when the bountifulness and love of God our Savior appeared. . . ." But if your spirits have not been as vile as some others, if they have been fair and ingenuous, if you have been of sweet natures and tractable dispositions, you have cause to bless God in some respects so much the more for the change He has wrought in them, for His mercy towards you, that you did not rest in those natural excellencies and mistake them for saving graces, as many do with much danger to their souls. And when you see the base, corrupt spirits of other men, as those who have anything to do in the world, shall meet with exceedingly vile, corrupt spirits; not only in the worst sort of men, but in those who seem to be fair, in whom a man would never have thought to have met with such base workings of spirit, that would make a man wonder, "O Lord, what are the spirits of men?" Then, I say, when you see this, bless the Lord. Let your spirits, and all that is within them, bless His name who has put such a difference between your spirits and theirs. And this you cannot but acknowledge unless you should be exceedingly injurious to the grace of God in you.

# Chapter Nine

# Communion and Conversation with Men of Such Excellent Spirits Is a Most Blessed Thing

*I*f the godly are of such excellent spirits, then conversation and communion with them is a most blessed thing. There is no greater heaven upon earth than this, for here you may see the beauty and luster of God's graces shining, the brightness of which darkens all the beauty and glory of the world to a spiritual eye. Seneca saw so much excellency put upon a man by morality that he said that "the very looks of a good man delight one." The very sight of such servants of God, who walk close with God, who are careful to keep their spirits clear and shining, truly is very delightful. It has much quickening in it. The uprightness, holiness, and spiritual enlightenments that their souls have will guide them to advise for God in safe and good ways.

The advice of godly men in things concerning God is much to be prized. It was a good speech of Shechaniah to Ezra, chapter 10:3: "Now therefore let us make a covenant with our

God . . . according to the counsel of the Lord, and of those that fear the commandments of our God." It was good to follow their counsel. The spirits of these are savory in their discourse, in their duties, in all their carriage; their example is exceedingly powerful and profitable. The blessing of Abigail upon David was: "The Lord bind up his soul in the bundle of life." Enjoyment of communion with God's people is the binding up of our souls in the bundle of life, for every one of them has life in Him. Doctor Taylor, the martyr, rejoiced that ever he came into prison because he came there to have acquaintance with that angel of God, John Bradford, as he called him. If the society of one sweet, heavenly-spirited man is enough to make a prison cheerful, what a blessing then is the enjoyment of communion with many?

"All my delight is the saints, in them that excel in the earth," said David. It is the blessing of the gospel to come to the spirits of just men made perfect (Hebrews 12:23). When we are among them, we may, in beholding the work of their spirits, come to see many failings in our own that we did not see before, and so be humbled for them and seek help. We may see the same graces shining in them that we feel in our own hearts, and be strengthened and encouraged in them and stirred up to bless God for them. The suitableness between their spirits and ours, if ours are right, will cause such a closing and mingling as from thence will arise an unspeakable delight and incomparable sweetness. No society under heaven has the pleasantness and sweetness in it as the society of the saints. No men's spirits close as fully with one another as theirs; no men's spirits are bound by such indissoluble bonds as theirs.

They know the excellency of one another's spirits so they can freely open themselves, unbosom their hearts one to another, and venture their lives one upon another. It is the most honorable society in the world, for it is the association of the most excellent and glorious creatures. God Himself delights to join Himself with them, to be among them. 2 Corinthians 6:16: "I will dwell among them," says the Lord, "and walk there, and I will be their God, and they shall be My people." But the words are more significant in the original. They express God's delight not only to dwell among them and walk with them, but to dwell *in* them and walk *in* them. Hence that expression of Tertullian that we used before is very pertinent for our purpose here: "When good men meet, when godly men are gathered together, this is not to be called a faction but a court." What place is accounted so honorable and excels in more delights than the courts of princes? The society of God's saints and communion with God's people has more honor, and is filled with more delights, than any court in the world where this is wanting.

The society of the wicked is unsavory and tedious because their spirits are so vile and corrupt, like the slime and filth that are congealed when many toads and venomous filthy creatures join together. How abominable are their breathings together to a gracious spirit? How loathsome is the mixture of their spirits? In Zechariah 13:2 we have a promise that God will, in His due time, take away the unclean spirit out of the land, and oh, what a blessed time will that be! How happy would God's servants think themselves if they might be delivered from the noisomeness of corrupt, unclean spirits! Let us keep ourselves, what we can now, from mingling with them. We shall, within a while, be forever delivered from them.

# Chapter Ten

# All Those Whose Spirits God Has thus Distinguished Should Improve this Mercy by Not Walking as Other Men

If God has been merciful to you in giving you another spirit, improve this mercy. Show in all your ways that you are acted upon by another spirit. Let the renewed spirit guide you; let the beauty and excellency of it appear. "If we live in the Spirit, let us walk in the Spirit," said the apostle in Galatians 5:25. "The works of the flesh are manifest" (Galatians 5:19). Why should not the works of the Spirit be so too? God has beautified your spirits with His own image. In this He has honored you that you might honor Him in holding forth the beauty and excellency of His image. He has made you a peculiar people to the end that you might show forth the virtues of Him who has called you out of darkness into His marvelous light (1 Peter 2:9).

It is a dishonor to a parent, or any special friend, to hang his picture in some dark hole, in some obscure, contemptible place. It is expected we should make it conspicuous, that we should hang it in some eminent place so as to manifest that we rejoice in it as an ornament to us. It is a great evil to obscure the graces of God's Spirit, to keep in the work of God upon our spirits in which He has set out the glory of His image, to the end that He might be glorified in us before men and angels. Every man delights in the expression of that wherein He esteems his excellency to consist, be it eloquence, wisdom, or any art wherein he has attained any eminence. Yea, if he accounts his excellency to consist in his riches, in his honor, in his beauty, he loves to make them appear before others as did the prophet in another case, Isaiah 60:1: "Arise and shine, for the light is come, and the glory of the Lord is risen upon thee." If God has shone upon your spirits by His grace, let your lights shine before men that the world may see there are men of other spirits who can do such things as they cannot. Oh, what beautiful, convincing conversations would men have if they were only acted upon by this renewed spirit! As it was said of Stephen, that they could not resist the spirit by which he spoke, so it would be true here. Men could not resist that spirit by which you live. "What do you more than other men?" said Christ to His disciples in Matthew 5:47. Men of other spirits must manifest in their lives that they can do more than other men. Let me, in the name of the Lord, plead with you for more honor and service for the Lord than He has from others.

1. Your birth is from Him. You are born of God in another manner than others are, and therefore it must not be with you as it is with others. Men of high birth will not live as other men do. Hence we read of a custom among the heathen: they were wont to derive the pedigree of their valiant men from their gods. To this end, though the thing was not true, yet they, believing themselves to be a divine offspring, might upon confidence thereof undertake higher attempts than others with more

boldness. Much higher things should those endeavor after who are indeed born of God.

2. God has put forth another manner of power out upon your spirits than upon other men. Other men have but a general common influence of God's power let into their spirits, but He has manifested the exceeding greatness of His power in you. Observe the gradation in Ephesians 1:19–20: the apostle, speaking of the power of God put forth upon those who believe, expresses it in a sixfold gradation:

(1) It is His power; only the power of a God could do it.

(2) It is the greatness of His power.

(3) It is the exceeding greatness of His power.

(4) It is the working of His power.

(5) It is the working of His mighty power.

(6) It is the same power by which He raised Christ from the dead and set Him at His right hand in the heavens, far above all principality, and power, and might. Now God does not usually put forth great power but for great purposes. He does not use His extraordinary power for ordinary things; when supernatural power is put forth it is that it might rise to supernatural operations.

3. Again, God puts other abilities into you that others have not. That grace with which He has endued your spirits is a spark of His own divine nature; as you have heard, it has a divine power *with* it and a divine activity *in* it. That is expected from you which none can do by an inferior power, as by the strength of parts, education, and moral principles. If your life is not beyond the highest of those who have no other principles than such to raise them, you dishonor God, His grace, and your holy profession.

4. Your spirits have been made acquainted with more truths. God has revealed to you the secrets of His counsels, of His kingdom. He has shown you Himself, His glory, His majesty,

sovereignty, and holiness. He has shown you the reality, beauty, excellency, and equity of His blessed ways. He has made known to you the certainty, the infinite consequence of the things of eternity; the vileness, pollution, poison, and danger of sin. He has given you experiences of the things of heaven, the sweetness of His ways, and the distress of conscience for sin.

5. He has separated you for Himself. He has taken you into a near communion unto Himself. Though God is to be feared by all, yet more especially in a higher degree He is to be feared in the assembly of His saints, and to be had in reverence of those who are about Him (Psalm 89:7).

6. God has put other dignities upon you that He has not put upon other men. He has made you citizens of the New Jerusalem, favorites of heaven, heirs, co-heirs with the Lord Jesus Christ. God has raised you above the condition of men, and therefore you must not walk as men. The apostle, in 1 Corinthians 3:3, blamed the Corinthians that they walked as men. "He hath redeemed you from the earth" (Revelation 14:3). Therefore, you must not walk as the men of the earth. God has not dealt thus with other people; they do not know what these things mean. Therefore, well may the Lord expect from you other manner of service and honor than He has from other men.

7. More depends upon you than upon others. The weight of many services depends all upon you that are in no way expected to be performed by others. What shall become of God's name, His glory, and the fulfilling of His will in the world if men whose spirits are fitted for this service should not live in a higher way of holiness, and do more for Him than others? God expects great things from you. Isaiah 63:8: "I said, surely they will not lie." Vile in their ways, yet God rejoices in this, that He has a generation in the world, a choice company of other spirits, pre-

cious and excellent spirits, and He shall have other dealings from them.

8. Your sins go nearer to the heart of God than others. Other men may provoke God to anger, but you grieve His Holy Spirit. God took it very ill at Solomon's hand that he dealt ill with Him after He had appeared twice to him (1 Kings 11:9). How often has God appeared to your souls? What gracious visitations have your spirits had from Him? It is a shameful thing indeed for you to fall as other men do. It was an aggravation of the fall of Saul (2 Samuel 1:21), that the shield of the mighty was cast down, the shield of Saul, as though he had not been anointed with oil. For you to fall as though you had not been anointed, as others who have no such ointment poured upon them, is a great and sore evil.

9. The eyes of many are upon you. The name of God, the cause of God is engaged in you.

10. You are appointed by God to be the judges of other men. 1 Corinthians 6:2: "Do you not know that the saints shall judge the world?" Yea, verse 3: "Know you not that we shall judge the angels?" God will bring your lives and ways before all the world to judge the world by, and therefore they need to be very exact, and to have something in them more than ordinary. It is a shameful way of reasoning for any man to reason for sin by example, as if, like a thief, he would fain escape in the crowd. But much more shameful is it that any godly man should be found to argue for sin this way, for this is an aggravation of sin, not a lessening of it. It is as if I should say, "God has dishonor by such and such, and therefore why may He not have some more by me?" Sin is a striking at God, and every sinner strikes at Him, and you come running for your stroke too. What? Will you also have your blow at Him, you for whom the Lord has done such great things?

As Caesar said to Brutus, when in the Senatehouse, the senators had wounded him with many sore wounds and Brutus came also for his stroke; "What? And thou my son, Brutus too?" Think of it as if you saw the Lord looking on you and saying that to you when you venture upon any sinful way by following the example of others.

QUESTION. But in what particulars should we manifest this choiceness of our spirits in ways differing from others?

ANSWER. In these especially:

1. In self-denial. Show that you can deny your opinions, your desires, and your wills. Though you have a strong desire for a thing, though you have fit opportunities to enjoy your desires, yet if you see God may have more honor in any other way, you can freely and readily, without disturbance, without vexing yield. And do not deceive yourselves in this. Be easily convinced in particulars that are for God and against yourselves. The excellency of a man's spirit is much seen in this.

Many think it an excellency of spirit to be self-willed, in the sense of passionate, froward, and boisterous. Certainly this comes from weakness of spirit. No excellency is required for this; every fool can be thus. But it is excellency to be able to overcome, to have command of one's spirit, to subdue and bring in order passions and violent stirrings of spirits. This is precious and honorable in the eyes of God and man. This is a well-tempered spirit indeed that can be strong, zealous, full of courage, and unyielding in the cause of God and the Church, but meek, quiet, yielding, and self-denying in its own cause. Those who usually are the most boisterous and passionate for themselves are the most poor-spirited men, and the most basely yielding when it comes to the cause of God.

2. Show the excellency of your spirit's enabling you to do

that which others cannot do by loving your enemies, praying for them, and doing them all the good you can. This is the special thing our Savior commands His disciples in Matthew 5 when He would have them do more than others do.

3. Fear the least sin more than the greatest suffering. Morality raises the spirit highest next to grace, and yet mere moral man accounts it foolishness to be so nice as not to yield in little things for the avoiding of great sufferings. But a gracious spirit thinks the least truth of God worthy to be witnessed to by the loss of his dearest comforts, and suffering the greatest evils. Yea, he accounts suffering for small things the most honorable sufferings of all, as testifying to the greatest love. David's worthies showed their dearest love for him in venturing their lives to get him a little water.

4. Prize opportunities for service more than all outward contentments in the world. A gracious heart thinks it honor enough that God employs it. He is not only willing to go on in his work, though outward contentments come not in. But he esteems increased service for God so great a good that he accounts the lack of outward things made up in it: "Though I do not get as much by what I do as others, yet I bless God that I can go on in my work as cheerfully as others, for contentment is made up to me in that God will employ me in His service more than others."

5. Make conscience of time. This few do. Few regard the filling up of their time, their spirits having no excellency in them. They cannot make use of their time in any worthy employments for God to themselves or others; but a man of an excellent spirit knows how to employ himself in things that are excellent, and therefore prizes the time he has to work in, and is conscientious in the spending of it.

6. Make conscience of thoughts and secret workings of

heart, of secret sins to avoid them and secret duties to perform them. A man who has a precious spirit does not like to have it run to waste in extravagant thoughts and affections. The thoughts of his mind are precious, and the affections of his heart are precious as his spirit is precious. We let water run to waste because we put no price upon it. We think it of little worth, and therefore we let it run to no use; but if it were some precious liquor, some precious oil, or compounded of dear ingredients we would not do so. We would be careful to save every drop. This is a precious-spirited man indeed who knows how to lay out his thoughts and his affections to the best advantage, and will not lavish them out to no purpose.

7. Make conscience of the *manner* of performing holy duties as well as of doing them; and look after them, what becomes of them when they are done. This is not according to the common spirits of the world, who think to put off God with flat, poor, and dead services. A gracious spirit has much of the excellency of his spirit acting in holy duties, and therefore he much minds them and looks much after them. But others have little of their spirits acting in them, and therefore they are little regarded, little looked after by them.

8. Rejoice in the good of others, though it eclipses your light, though it makes your parts, your abilities, and your excellencies dimmer in the eyes of others. Were it not for the eminence of some above you, your parts perhaps would shine brightly and be of high esteem. Yet to rejoice in this from the heart, to bless God from the soul for His gifts and graces in others, that His name may be glorified more by others than I can glorify it myself; to be able truly to say, "Though I can do little, yet blessed be God there are some who can do more for God than I, and in this I do and will rejoice"—this is indeed to be able to do much more than others. This shows a great emi-

nence of spirit. All the parts, gifts, and abilities that any man in the world has, where this property is not present, they come far short of this excellency. To be able to do this is more than to be able to excel others in any excellency whatsoever. If God has given you this, He has given you that which is a thousand times more worthy than strong parts and abilities, in which you might have been far more eminent than you now are or than others are.

9.  If you will show the excellency of this spirit in some choice thing, then labor to keep the heart low in prosperity, and full of heavenly cheerfulness in adversity. Be not only contented but joyful in a quiet, sweet, delightful frame. In the greatest difficulties and straits, when you are put upon hard things, go on in your way with what strength you can, without vexing, distracting thoughts. Let your spirits be stayed on God, quietly and meekly committing yourselves and your cause to Him, as did the people of God in Isaiah 26:8. They professed their willingness in all quietness to wait upon God in the ways of His judgments, and they give this reason, that "the desire of their soul is to His name, and to the remembrance of Him."

If in the times of our troubles the desires of our souls were to God's name and the remembrance of Him, and not unto our own names and the remembrance of ourselves, we would not have such sinking, discouraged, disquieted, and vexing spirits as we have. The spirits of most men, if any difficult thing befalls them, are presently in a hurry, so disquieted and tumultuous that all the peace and sweetness of them are lost. And they hinder themselves exceedingly both in the business they are about, adding much to the difficulty of it, and in all other businesses that concern them. This notes much distemper of spirit, like distempered flesh of a man's body; if it is but touched with the finger or the least air come to it, it presently festers and rankles.

10. Be more careful to know the fountain from whence all your mercies come, and to have a sanctified use of them when you enjoy them, than to have the possession of them or delight in them. An ordinary spirit looks at nothing but to have the things it desires. It is not solicitous about the fountain from whence they spring, nor careful to attain any sanctified end to which they tend. It looks not at them as from God, neither uses them for God; but where all these are, here is the work of a choice, precious spirit, indeed, the peculiar work of it. This is to do more than others, and thus God's servants must do or else they can never live convincing lives.

While Pharaoh and his magicians saw that Moses did no more than they could do, they were not convinced; but when Moses did that which they could not do, then they acknowledged the finger of God. So it is here. While wicked men see those who are religious do only such things as they could do if they would—as going to sermons or speaking of good things—they are never convinced by them. But when they see them do something which their consciences tell them they cannot do, then they are forced to acknowledge that there is a real excellency in godliness which they have not. Christ said once, "If I had not done those things that no man did, they had not had sin" (John 15:24). It aggravated the sin of the Jews that they did not believe in Christ, notwithstanding He did those works among them no man ever did.

So, if godly men manifested the choiceness of their spirits among the men of the world in doing such as no other can do, this, if it did not convert them and bring them in love with God's ways, would certainly aggravate their sin and increase their condemnation. It is therefore a most shameful thing that those who make a great show and profession of godliness should in their lives be no more than equal unto, yea, be lower than others who are merely moral—lower than a Socrates, than a Fabritius, than others of the heathen.

How many civil, moral men go beyond them who would be taken for godly? They are more meek and patient, more courteous, more faithful and trusty, more liberal and helpful, more ingenuous and candid. Many servants who would seem godly are not as obedient, as diligent, as humble and submissive, as conscionable in their work as others whom they judge merely carnal. So, many wives do not behave with that quietness, respect, love, and obedience to their husbands as others whom they themselves judge to be only civil. In like manner, many husbands and masters of their families profess godliness yet in their houses are more froward, more dogged, more churlish, cruel, and bitter to wife and servants than others whom they esteem only carnal. Many children are more stout to their parents, and parents more negligent in the care they ought to have of their children, than others.

What a shame is it, said Saint Jerome, that faith should not be able to do that which infidelity has done. What? Not better fruit in the garden, in the vineyard of the Lord, than in the wilderness? What? Not better fruit growing upon the tree of life than upon the root of nature? Where does the power of godliness lie? If it does not carry men beyond these, what is it to live godly in Christ? What are the virtue, the power, and the life of Christ, if they do not enable one to go beyond others? There is needed no such virtue, power, or life of Christ Jesus to enable one to do that which others can do. What? Is godliness but a notion, but a conceit, that it will not carry men beyond the light of nature?

# CHAPTER ELEVEN

# An Exhortation to Labor to Get this Excellent Spirit

USE OF EXHORTATION. Let us labor to get this other spirit. Everyone desires to be eminent, to be above others in estate, in esteem, in natural excellencies. If we would be eminent, let us labor to be eminent in spiritual blessings, in getting our souls endued with higher spiritual excellencies than others have. It is commendable to strive to be as eminent here as we can, especially you whom God has raised higher than your brethren in other things—in the nobility of your births, the eminence of your places, the greatness of your estates. Do you labor to be high above others in the excellencies of your spirits, that as your birth is other, your places other, your estate other than common men's, so your spirits may be other spirits? What an excellent thing is it to have a spirit suitable to one's condition! "A great mind becomes a great fortune," said Seneca. He means greatness of mind in the exercise of virtue, which alone gives a true greatness to the mind. I know this is a powerful argument with you to make grace lovely and desirable in your eyes, to tell you that it will raise your spirits, that it will put beauty and glory upon them, that it will add greatness and excellency to them.

The world is much for brave spirits; we desire yours may be

so. Only mistake not the true nobleness, the true excellency of spirit. Certainly it is in that which may bring you nearest to God, the highest excellency. You can in no way be so honorable as by the raising of your spirits by grace. Wisdom with an inheritance is good; wisdom with birth and eminence of place is a great blessing indeed. To be rich in goods and rich in goodness is a happy connection. You would account it a great disgrace not to have education somewhat suitable to your birth and quality. What can be more dishonorable of a man than this: "He has been left indeed a great estate, and is of a great house, but he has no breeding?" What? Is a competent measure of knowledge in tongues and arts, and other things suitable to your births and estates, accounted a beauty and ornament to them, and are not grace and godliness much more? Do these add an excellency to your quality and put an honor upon your dignities, and will not godliness much more? Shall sea and land be traveled over with much hazard of soul and body, with great expense of estate, to get knowledge of fashions, and a gentle behavior, because you think they will be ornaments to your great estates you were born to; and shall no labor be undertaken to get godliness, to get your spirits raised by grace as an ornament to the greatness of your birth and eminence of your estate? How this slights the very glory of God Himself, and condemns the highest dignity men and angels are capable of!

Are any places so fit for wisdom as the high places of the city? Proverbs 9:1, 3: "Wisdom hath builded her house, she hath hewn out her seven pillars, she crieth upon the highest places of the city." How honorable does godliness make those whose birth, whose place is honorable in the eyes of God, His saints, blessed angels, and in the consciences of all! How well does grace suit with the highest dignity, as a bright shining diamond in a golden ring! As the world is drawn more conspicuous and full in a large map than in a small, so the beauty and excellency of grace and godliness appear more conspicuous and glorious in great and honorable men than in those who are of a meaner rank.

1. You need other spirits more than other persons for the improvement of those great mercies that you have above others. As some fowl that have great wings yet can fly but little, so many men have great estates, but, not having spirits to improve them, they are of little use. Know that your estates are either mercies or miseries, blessings or cursings to you, according as you have hearts to improve them. If they are improved for God, as advantages to honor God by, to do good with, they are great blessings then indeed. And that is as great an argument of the truth of grace as any, to be as earnest with God for a heart to improve an estate or a place of dignity for God as to rejoice that you have such an estate for yourselves, or that you are in such an eminent place whereby you may get honor for yourselves. Where God gives not a more excellent spirit than others, an eminent estate is made but as fuel to nourish and maintain all manner of evil, to afford opportunities for acting out sin. And is not this the excellency that many account to be in their estates in that it is higher than others, in that they can have their wills and satisfy their lusts more than others?

2. You need other spirits for the improving of the large opportunities of service for God and His Church that you have more than others do. These are as great blessings as your estates or any dignities you have above others. God entrusts you with much in giving you such large opportunities of service for the honor of His great name. If your birth is high, your estates high, and your spirits endued with excellency from on high, how fit then are you to be used by God in high and honorable services? Hence the conversion of a great man is of exceedingly great consequence. Whereupon Saint Paul was so loath

to lose the conversion of the deputy Sergius Paulus who began to listen to his preaching, of whom we read in Acts 13:8–11: "Therefore when Elymas withstood him in this work, seeking to turn away the deputy from the faith, the spirit of Saint Paul rose against him with much indignation; and being filled with the Holy Ghost he set his eyes on him and said, 'O full of all subtlety and all mischief, thou child of the Devil, thou enemy of righteousness, wilt thou not cease to pervert the right ways of the Lord? And now, behold, the hand of the Lord is upon thee, and thou shalt be blind.' "

It is as if St. Paul had said, "What? Will you hinder men in such a great work as this wherein God may have so much honor in the conversion of this noble man, this man of public and eminent place? This indeed is to be full of all mischief, to be an enemy of all righteousness." Thus you see how his spirit was stirred when he was put in fear of being hindered in such a notable prize as this. This is as when a man is likely to have a great draft, there comes in one who disturbs him and is likely to hinder him from having it. Surely Paul saw that it was a wonderful great blessing to the Church to have great men brought into the obedience of the faith and added to it.

And it is further observed that God, going along with Paul and finishing the work of the conversion of this great man, changed his name from Saul and called him Paulus, from that notable work of the conversion of this Sergius Paulus. Many great captains among the heathen were wont to have their names changed upon their success in some noble enterprise and great victories. Scipio Africanus was called Africanus from his conquest of Africa.

3. You who are in high and eminent dignities, you are the subject of the earnest prayers of God's servants in all places, that God would raise you up with truly noble, excellent, and gracious

spirits, that you may be instruments of His glory. How blessed you are if God fulfills the prayers of His servants upon you! What great pity is it that such blessed opportunities of service, of honoring God, themselves, and families as you have should be lost for want of spirits! Would it not more honorable to you and your household to be employed as public blessings to Church and Commonwealth, to have thousands of souls bless you and bless God for you, than for you to go finer than others, to have your tables better furnished than others, to sport and game more than others, to spend more than others?

4. Again, you need other spirits, for your example is looked at more than others, either in good or evil. As Christ said of Himself in another case, "If I be lifted up, I will draw all men after Me"; so I may say, if godliness is lifted up in the examples of great ones, it will draw all men after it. Whatever evil is seen in you is not only followed by others, but used as a plea to maintain and encourage that which is evil in many others. Charles V was wont to say that as the eclipse of the sun is a fore-token of great commotion, so the errors and oversights of great men bring with them great perturbations to the places where they live.

5. Their sin is worse than others for it does more hurt, and therefore their punishment will be greater than others. As their actions are exemplary, so will their punishments be. Hence that place in Micah 6:5: "O my people, remember what Balak consulted, and from Shittim unto Gilgal"; at Shittim the Lord destroyed the heads of the people (Numbers 25:4). The destruction of great ones is to be forever remembered.

6. And yet further, you need other spirits because you have temptations greater and stronger than others have. Therefore, if you have not the more excellent spirits, you are in greater danger than others. The high estate of great, outward dignity is a very dangerous estate, if God gives not an extraordinary

spirit. There is a notable story of Pius V, that Pope who excommunicated Queen Elizabeth. My author of the story is a Jesuit, Cornelius á Lapide, one highly esteemed amongst the Papists; and therefore the truth of it is to be the less suspected. The story is this: he says that this Pope was wont to say of himself, "When I was first in religious orders (that is, without any further ecclesiastical dignity) I had a very good hope of the salvation of my soul; but being made a Cardinal I began to be much afraid. But now being Pope, I do even despair." So, says Cornelius, did Clement VIII, who followed after him, think of himself. Thus by this example we see what a dangerous thing it is to be raised in outward honor, if yet still the spirit continues base and vile.

7. Above all, you who are honorable and great in the world need to labor to be gracious, because sin is more unsuitable to your condition than to others. It was the complaint of the Church (Lamentations 4:5), that those who were brought up in scarlet embraced the dung. How unsuitable was this, to have the highest places and the lowest spirits! Bernard, writing to a noble virgin who was godly, said that "others were clothed with purple and silk, but their consciences were poor and beggarly; they glistened with their jewels, but were base in their manners; but you," says he, "without are meanly clad, but within shine exceedingly beautiful, not to human but to divine eyes." How unsuitable was the one, but how comely and suitable the other.

It is reported of Scipio Africanus that when he took new Carthage, he took a young gentlewoman prisoner who was so fair that she ravished all men's eyes. Scipio then said, "If I were but a common soldier I would enjoy this damsel, but being commander of an army I will not meddle with her." And so preserving her entire he restored her to her friends. Thus he, though a heathen, thought wickedness too mean for, and unsuitable to, greatness. Sin is uncomely anywhere, much more uncomely among great ones; and grace is comely wherever it is, much more to the great ones of the earth. As Aeneas Sylvius was wont to say concerning learning, I may say the same concerning godliness: popular men should esteem learning as silver, noble men should account it like gold, and princes should prize it like pearls. Thus if godliness is as silver to ordinary men, it is to be accounted as gold and pearls to you. The Scripture compares beauty in a woman without wisdom to a pearl in a swine's snout (Proverbs 11:22), an unsuitable thing. Thus are all outward excellencies where there is no grace.

8. And would it not be a grievous thing to you to see poor, inferior, mean men and women lifted up to glory, and yourselves cast out with an eternal curse? Have not many of them most excellent, precious spirits? Do they not do God far more service than you? Do they not bring more honor to His name than ever you did? Think then with yourselves, "Why should God put those who are of such choice, precious spirits into such a low condition, and raise me to such a high one? Is it not because He intends to give me my portion in life, but reserves better mercies for them afterwards?" It would be very grievous indeed if it should prove so.

9. The hopes we have of the continuance of our peace in the happy enjoyment of those precious liberties of the gospel, that in so great mercy have been continued unto us, depend much upon the work of God's grace upon your souls. If God takes off your spirits from common vanities, from the pleasures of the flesh, from the poor low things of the world, from your own private ends, and causes the fear of His great name to fall upon them, and raises them to the love of, and delight in, the great things of godliness, to be given up wholly to Him and to lift up His great name—we shall then look upon you as the joyful hopes of our souls, that God still does and will delight in

the blessing, peace, and prosperity of His people. But if we see darkness upon your spirits, then a dismal night of darkness is upon us.

When we see it wax dark in the valleys, we say it is towards night. If it begins to be dark upon the hills it is near night; but if it is dark in the sky it is night indeed. So where we see the works of darkness among the people, it is a sign that a night is coming; but where we see them in those of a higher rank, in the gentry, it makes us fear that the night is nearer. But if they are in the nobility and the great men, then it is a dismal night indeed.

Wherefore be exhorted in the name of the Lord to labor much that you may have more gracious and holy spirits than others, together with your dignities whereby you are lifted up above others. We envy not your honors; we desire that they may be raised higher by grace. Grace may well stand with the enjoyment of all your dignities, yea, grace is the only thing that blesses and advances them.

And you whose spirits God has raised above others in the excellencies of your parts, and who have many excellent endowments of learning, who are men of larger understandings, of higher apprehensions than others and can look upon ordinary men as low and mean with respect to difference is between your parts and theirs, do you labor yet to raise your spirits higher by grace and godliness, that as you differ from them in natural excellencies, so you may differ from them much more in spiritual and divine ones? How eminent would you be in grace if those parts and abilities of learning you have were sanctified for God! What blessed instruments might you be of glory to God, of comfort and encouragement to His people! But otherwise your parts and gifts are poisoned; and a sinful, wicked heart will poison all. It may be said of many, as it was of Pope Eugenius II—he

was a man of great learning and great eloquence with a mixture of great hypocrisy, if it may be thus said of any. He was a
man indeed of excellent parts, very learned, of strong abilities,
but he had a corrupt spirit. He was a man of a corrupt mind.
Surely these parts were all poisoned, and it is no marvel, then,
if such men swell so much by reason of them. Parts unsancti-
fied exceedingly enlarge men's spirits, to be so much the more
capable of spiritual wickedness, more than others of meaner
and lower parts can be. Your parts will aggravate all your sins
and increase your damnation. It is a lamentable thing that such
excellent parts and abilities as many have, which might be of so
great use for God and His Church, should vanish into froth.

Such was the great complaint of one Robertus Gallus, a
famous man, an opposer of the corruptions of those times in
which he lived, which was the 13th century. He compared the
school doctors to one having bread and good wine hanging on
both his sides; yet, notwithstanding, who was gnawing hungrily
on a flint stone. Thus they, leaving the wholesome food in the
Scriptures, busied themselves with subtle questions wherein
there was no edification or comfort to the soul. Thus their
excellent parts all vanished into nothing. Now if it is so grievous
a thing for parts and learning to be employed about mean and
unworthy things, how much more grievous is it when they are
employed against God! Oh, what great cause we have then to
pray for these men whose spirits are raised by natural parts!
And how great cause have they themselves to seek God, and to
use all means that their spirits might be likewise raised by grace,
that great blessings of parts and learning might come to them
by God's bestowing upon them this other spirit! Oh, consider
what an opprobious thing it is to you that God should have
more fear, honor, and service from men of lower, far meaner,
weaker abilities; that their hearts should close more with the

ways of godliness; that their hearts should be more enlarged towards God than yours; that they should enjoy more heavenly, spiritual communion with God than you, yea, such communion with God as you are altogether unacquainted with; and that at length their souls should be saved and forever blessed when yours shall be cast out as filth, and as an everlasting abhorrence, from the presence of the Lord. What a grievous thing will it be to you when it shall appear that your parts shall serve for no other end than to enlarge your souls to be more capable of the wrath of God than other men! For be assured that none are so filled with God's wrath as knowing men.

This was the grievous complaint of Saint Augustine in his time: "The unlearned rise up and take heaven by force, and we with all our learning are thrust down into hell." It is a speech well known to scholars. Of how great use might it be, if God settled it upon their hearts? And Saint Bernard had a speech somewhat similar: "Let the wise of the world, who mind high things and yet feed upon the earth, let them with their wisdom go down into hell." And Luther had a notable story that may be very useful for this purpose. It is in his writings upon the Fourth Commandment, which he makes the third. It is to show how the holiness of the spirits of mean and unlearned men shall confound learned men of great understanding who do not have the like godliness.

In the time of the Council of Constance, Luther says, "There were two Cardinals riding to the Council, and in their journey they saw a shepherd in the field weeping. One of them, pitying him, said that he could not pass by, but he must go to yonder man and comfort him. Coming near to him, he asked him why he wept. He was loath to tell him at first; but being urged he told him, saying, 'I, looking upon this toad, considered that I had never praised God as I ought for making me such an excellent creature as a man, comely and reasonable. I have not blessed Him that He made not me such a deformed toad as this.' When the Cardinal heard this, he was struck with it, considering that he had received greater mercies than this poor man. And he was so struck that he fell down presently dead from his mule. His servants lifted him up and brought him to the city. He came to life again and then cried out: 'Oh, Saint Augustine, how truly didst thou say, "The unlearned rise, and they take heaven, and we with all our learning wallow in flesh and blood!" ' "

You, therefore, whom God has honored with excellent parts, that you may not be thus confounded another day before the Lord and His blessed angels and saints, be restless in your spirits till you find God has added a further beauty to them, even the beauty of holiness, the sanctifying graces of His Holy Spirit, that may make you lovely in His eyes, truly honorable before Him, and forever blessed of Him. Take heed you rest neither in gifts of learning or in gifts of morality. The gifts of morality are yet a further ornament to men's spirits, but they come short of those divine excellencies of spirit that will make it blessed forever.

We read of many who were very eminent in moral excellencies and yet altogether strangers to the life of grace. For example, Josephus reports of Herod the king that which would make one think he was raised to very high moral excellencies. Once, making a speech to his army, among other passages he had this: "Perhaps some men will say that right and equity are on our side, but that the greater number of men and means are with the other; but this speech is unworthy of my followers: for with those with whom justice is, with those also God is; and where God is, there neither wants multitude nor fortitude."

And he reports of him that in the time of a famine he caused all his vessels of gold and silver to be melted to buy corn for the relief of the poor. That Herod likewise, which St. Luke speaks of in Acts 12:23, who was smote by the angel and eaten by worms, yet even this man had many excellent moral gifts. Josephus reported of him that he was a man of a most mild disposition, ready to help those who were in adversity, free from outward gross defilements, and that no day passed him in which he did not offer sacrifice. And for a testimony of his mild and gentle temper Josephus told a notable story. One Simon, a lawyer, in his absence had scandalized him with many grievous accusations before the people. He was a profane man, and upon just cause he was forbidden to enter the temple. When Herod was certified of these things, and came to the theater, he commanded that this Simon should be brought to him, and would have him sit down next to him. In a peaceable and kind manner he spoke thus to him: "Tell me, I pray thee, what thing seest thou fault-worthy or contrary to the Law in me?" This Simon, not having anything to answer, sought his pardon. The king grew friends with him and dismissed him, bestowing gifts on him. What a shame is this example to many Christians! And yet we would all be loath to be in this man's condition.

It is reported likewise of Titus, whom God made a grievous scourge to the Jews, that yet he was so meek, so liberal, so merciful, of so mild and sweet a nature, that he was usually called "the love and delight of mankind." If he had done no good in any day, he would say, "I have lost this day." Suetonius tells of him that he was wont to use this speech, that "none should go away sad from speaking with a prince."

Excellent things are likewise reported of Trajan. He was accounted a pattern of upright dealing, inasmuch as when a new emperor was afterwards elected the people were wont to wish him the good success of Augustus and the uprightness of

Trajan. And yet the persecution of Christians under him was very grievous. It is likewise said of Antonius Philosophus that he was of such a sweet temper that he was never much puffed up in prosperity nor cast down in adversity.

Thus we see that men may have excellent gifts of morality, and yet all these are but as flowers that grow on brambles, far different from those graces of this other spirit that we speak of which only grows upon the tree of life. As many a fair flower may grow out of a stinking root, so many sweet dispositions and fair actions may be where there is only the corrupt root of nature. It is true, learning and morality are lovely; they are pearls highly to be esteemed; they are great blessings of God. But there is a pearl of price which is beyond them all which the true wise merchant will labor to get and will be content to sell all to obtain, as in Matthew 13:45–46. And this pearl of price is that by which this other spirit comes to be so excellent above all that learning and morality or any common gifts can make it. It is said in Matthew that the wise merchant sought other goodly pearls. Common gifts are to be sought after as things that have much excellency in their kind, but it was that one pearl of great price that he sold all for. It is that grace of God in Christ that raises the spirit above all other excellencies, and is to be prized and sought after above all things whatsoever. And that you may know that there is a great deal of difference between natural endowments, moral virtues, and true spiritual excellencies, that this other spirit is far beyond natural excellencies, note these differences:

## How this other spirit surpasses natural excellencies

1. This other spirit is a renewed spirit. "A new spirit will I give you," said the Lord in Ezekiel 11:19. It does not arise out of

principles bred up with us; the Lord makes the spirit sensible of its natural corruption and weakness, and of the mighty work of His grace upon it. It is made another spirit by a high and super-natural work of God upon the soul, working a mighty change in it, creating new principles and new habits. Examine what change you have found in your spirits. If they are no other than ever have been, yea, if the change is only gradual, not essen-tial; if it is only the raising of some natural principles, so as to enable you to live in a somewhat fairer way than you did; if it is not the work of God breaking your spirits in pieces and making of them a new spirit; if it is not a new creation in you, surely, then, yet your spirits are void of that true blessed excellency that this other spirit has.

2. This other spirit works from God and for God. It is sen-sible of the need it has of continual influence from heaven; and it draws virtue and efficacy from God, conveying His grace to the soul through that blessed covenant that He has made with the children of men in Jesus Christ. And receiving this grace from on high, it is acted up to God Himself; it looks at God in what it does; it is carried out of love for Him with unfeigned desires to lift up His great name. Moral virtues are wrought by that reasonableness the soul sees in such virtuous actions, and the highest pitch they reach to is the love to that equity which appears in them to a man's reason. Therefore the spirit of a man that is raised no higher than these blesses itself rather than God in the exercise of them. It is far from drawing any vir-tue from God in a way of a covenant of grace, or from denying itself and returning all the praise and honor to God.

Seneca was a man of as brave a spirit of morality almost as ever lived; and yet see how far he was from working from God and for God. Observe a strange expression of his in one of his epistles: "The cause and foundation of a blessed life is to trust oneself, to be confident in oneself; it is a shameful thing to weary God in prayer for it. What needs prayer? Make thyself happy. It's a foolish thing to desire a good mind, when thou mayest have it from thyself: right reason is enough to fill up the happiness of a man."

3. Where true spiritual excellency is, there is a connection of all spiritual excellencies, of all graces. Ephesians 5:9: "The fruit of the Spirit is in all goodness and righteousness, and truth"; and the reason is that all are united in one root, namely in love for God and holiness. The beauty and comeliness that God puts upon the spirit in the work of grace is a perfect beauty and comeliness (Ezekiel 16:14). There is no grace wanting, there is all true spiritual blessings. Ephesians 1:3: "Blessed be God, who hath blessed us with all spiritual blessings." So the words are in your books, but in the original, "blessings" is in the singular number: "with all spiritual blessing." There is all, and yet it is but one blessing, to note that spiritual blessings are so knit together that they all make up but one blessing. And therefore, where there is one blessing truly, there none can be wanting. There is such grace as, in the growth of it, springs up to eternal life. There is such a perfection as wants only the ripening, and it would be the same with the life in heaven; but where there wants any essential part, though it is ripened never so much, let it grow up never so fast, it will never come to be perfect. Thus, if there is any work of grace wanting, if there is any defect in the principle, though that is there and grows up never so fast, yet it would never attain unto eternal life. Conversely, in the work of sanctification, where it is true, though it is never so weak, yet there is this perfection—that there are all graces in it. But where there is only a sweet nature, where there is only some moral work upon the spirit, there are only some particular excellencies. The most moral man who ever lived has

had some way of evil that his spirit has run out unto.

4. Where there are true spiritual excellencies, there is an impulse of heart, a strong bent of spirit, in following after the Lord. There is such a powerful impression of divine truths upon the soul as presses it on with strength in God's ways so that it cannot easily be hindered. In Isaiah 8:11, the Lord spoke to this prophet with a strong hand that he should not walk in the way of the people. Such a spirit has not only some desires for that which is good, but goes on bound in the spirit, as Paul said of himself that the love of Christ constrained him. There is a power of godliness where it is true. When Elijah had cast his mantle upon Elisha, the spirit of Elisha was pressed to follow him (1 Kings 19:19–20), so that when Elisha desired to leave him, to go to his father and mother to take his leave of them, and said that then he would follow him, Elijah answered him, "What have I done to thee?" Elijah indeed did nothing in outward appearance to draw him after him, for what was the casting of his mantle upon him to work such an effect in him? But together with the casting of his mantle, there went a spirit into Elisha that he could not but follow him. Such a powerful work is there in the sanctifying graces of God's Spirit that it comes with strength to cause the soul to follow Him. There is a law of the mind that has power and command in it, just as before there was a law of sin.

But where there are only sweet natures, there men are easily drawn one way, and as easily drawn the other way. They join with those who are good in good actions, but their hearts are not so set on what they do but that they may be easily taken off and carried another way.

5. Where there are only moral principles, there the soul sees not into, is not sensible of, turns not from the evil of sin as the greatest evil. It sees not such evil in it as to make it subscribe to the righteousness of God in all those dreadful things that

are threatened against it, but thinks they are too hard: "Surely, God is not so severe a God." God forbid things should be so for you as for those we read of in the gospel. Christ spoke that parable concerning those who smote the servants of the Lord of the vineyard, Luke 20:16, and told them that the Lord should come and destroy those husbandmen, and give his vineyard to others. It is said that when they heard that they said, "God forbid." So many, when they hear the dreadful wrath of God pronounced against sin, say, "God forbid"; they think indeed that sin ought not to be committed, but they do not think it so great an evil as to procure so great miseries. But if their spirits were right, they would apprehend sin as being opposed to an infinite good, and so having a kind of infiniteness of evil in it. They would not only yield to the justice of God revealed, but acknowledged that there are greater and more fearful miseries due to it than can be conceived. Yea, they would see cause that if God should bring those evils upon them for their sin, there is infinite equity that they should lay their hands upon their mouths and take shame to themselves and acknowledge the Lord to be righteous forever.

6. Where there are only natural and moral excellencies, they do not raise the soul to a love of the strictest ways of God. They think accuracy and exactness in God's ways to be but niceness and too much precision. Lukewarmness is the only temper suitable to them. They think wisdom consists in the remission of godliness, not in the improvement of it; and what is beyond their temper they judge as weakness and folly. And moral men must have such thoughts of the strictness of the ways of God because that good they have is such as arises from the principles of natural reason and makes natural good its end. Therefore, all their virtue and goodness must be such as must not stretch nature, but must be subservient to that natural good they frame

to themselves. Now observing some rules and duties of religion will suit well with this; and just so far they approve and think well of religion. And here they stick, thinking anything further than this is folly and more than needs be. The work of godliness, in its power, must be distasteful to them because it seeks to empty a man of himself, to cause him to deny himself, to fetch all from principles beyond himself, and to be for a higher good than he himself is, which is an infinite good. And therefore, if it were possible, the godly spirit would work infinitely towards this goal, and would not set limits on itself.

7. Where there is only nature or morality, there is not sense of the breathings of God's Spirit in His ordinances. The ordinances are dead and flat things to them. A mere moral man can like well enough of presenting himself in the ordinances, but he feels no virtue in them. There is no impression that they work upon him which abides on his spirit after the ordinances are done. He knows not what it is to enjoy God in them; he knows not what it is to stir up himself to take hold of God in the exercise of them. Those excellencies he has are not drawn out, maintained, or increased by spiritual objects and duties. But it is otherwise where true spiritual excellencies are. Such a one goes to ordinances and holy duties with an expectation of meeting with the Lord there. He can discern and feel the gracious presence of the Lord; he finds the Spirit of the Lord breathing graciously upon his spirit and refreshing his soul with much quickening, life, and sweetness. He finds his spirit drawn out by them, his heart much enlarged, his graces much increased in the use of them; or if at some times he wants this, then he is sensible of the want of it, of that difference that now he feels between that which sometimes he has had and that which now he wants. But the other is sensible of no such want; all times are alike with him.

Thus you see how you may examine your spirits, whether the excellencies of them are natural, whether they are only moral or truly spiritual. By these notes you may see that to be true of yourselves that our Savior said to His disciples in another case: "You know not what spirit you are." Though God has given you many excellent blessings, and beautified your spirits with many excellent endowments that are in themselves lovely and desirable, perhaps yet He has not raised your spirits to that true spiritual excellency that He raises the spirits of His people unto, even in this world. There are yet other higher excellencies to be attained to, to be sought after, without which all the other you have will vanish and never bring up your souls to the enjoyment of God as yours in Christ.

QUESTION. But what should be done that we may get another spirit?
ANSWER 1. Work what you can upon your hearts whatever truth may further convince you of the difference of spirits, that you may be thoroughly convinced that there is indeed a vast, essential difference, and that you may see into the evil of your spirits and be sensible of the want of this true spiritual excellency and lie down before God dejected and humbled in the sight thereof.

ANSWER 2. Be much in the company of the godly. When Saul was among the prophets, the Spirit of God came upon him and he began to prophesy too. Elijah told Elisha that if he were with him when he was taken up, then he would have his spirit come upon him. Wherefore Elisha kept close to him and would by no means leave his company. By being much in the company of the godly, you will come to see some beams of the excellency of their spirits shine out to you whereby you will see that your spirits are not like theirs; that they are in a happier condition than you; that they are men in a nearer reference to God than you. You will soon discern that surely the world is mistaken in its view of these men.

ANSWER 3. Frequent the ordinances of God where the Spirit usually breathes. Set your souls before the work of God's Spirit. The Spirit breathes where it will; therefore it must be attended upon in those ways which it chooses. Though your spirits are never so dead and polluted, who knows but at length, in attending upon God in His way, the Spirit of God may breathe upon you, may breathe in you the breath of life. It has breathed upon spirits as dead and polluted as yours, and it has cleansed and sanctified them. It has filled and sanctified them; it has filled them full of spiritual and glorious excellencies.

ANSWER 4. Nourish and make good use of those common works of God's Spirit you have already. They have much excellency in them, and if they are not rested in but improved, they may be very serviceable for the work of God's grace. But as Christ says of the riches of the world, "If you are not faithful in them, who will trust you with the true riches?" So, if you are not careful to make use of the common works of God's Spirit, how can it be expected that the Lord should bless you with further mercy in this way? Be sure you do not willfully go against the rules of right reason you are convinced of. Do not darken that light of reason that God has set up in you. Do not extinguish those sparks in natural conscience that God has kindled there. Do not dread those principles you have received in your education. Use that strength of reason, resolution, and natural conscience you have to keep in your spirits that they are not let out to feed upon sinful delights.

With what face can you complain of weakness and yet feed your distempers? There is little hope for such as have extinguished the light of their common principles, which once they had in an eminent manner. Their light of reason once was at least as a fair candlelight, but now it is like the snuff in a socket, almost drowned and quenched with their filthy lusts. How just with God would it be that these men should be left to die and perish forever in their filth!

ANSWER 5. Seek God earnestly to renew and sanctify your spirits. It is He who is the Father of spirits; and the spirit of man is under no other power, but the power of God Himself. He has the command of all, and with Him there is abundance of spirit. He is willing, yea, He has promised to give His Spirit to those who ask it (Luke 11:13).

But you will say, "How can I pray without the Spirit?"

I answer, put yourself upon prayer, and who knows but assistance and blessing may come? Present yourself before the Lord. Tell Him what you apprehend of the vileness and filthiness of your spirit, what convictions you have of the need to renew it, of the excellency you see in the spirits of His servants. Tell Him of those desires you have to be blessed with such a spirit: "O Lord, Thou hast given me many bodily blessings, great blessing of my estate more than others, many excellent gifts. But Lord, there are other mercies my soul wants. Oh, that Thou wouldest give me another spirit!" As Caleb (Joshua 15:19), gave his daughter Achsah a blessing, namely the upper springs and the nether springs, so should you seek God that, as He has given you the blessing of the nether springs, so He may give you the blessing of the upper—namely that He may bless your soul with true spiritual blessings.

ANSWER 6. Be sure you look up to God in Christ, to seek this mercy in Him. Look on Him as anointed by the Father with the fullness of the Spirit. Look to Him in whom all the fullness of the Godhead dwells bodily, that out of this fullness spiritual blessings may be conveyed to you; for otherwise whatever you seek from God, but not in this way, you seek for only in a natural way.

ANSWER 7. Be careful to observe the beginnings of those special stirrings of God's Spirit in you, those gales that sometimes you may feel, and then put on what possibly you can. Then follow the work of God's grace; make much of such beginnings; give yourself up to their power. Turn motions of God's Spirit into purposes, and those purposes into endeavors, and those endeavors into performances, and seek that those performances may be established. We do not know what we lose when at any time we lose the stirrings of God's Spirit in our hearts. Who knows but that your eternal estate may depend upon those sparks that He is now kindling in you? It is a great wickedness to stifle the child in the womb when it is newly conceived, and is it not a great wickedness to stifle those blessed motions that are conceived by the work of the Holy Ghost? And for a conclusion of this point, let your spirit be forever restless until you feel God graciously coming in to you. Let no mercy satisfy you till God gives you soul-mercies, and blesses you with His choice spiritual blessings, such as are peculiar to those who are good in His eyes.

# PART 2

## A Gracious Spirit Follows God Fully

---

*...and hath followed me fully,*
*him will I bring into the land, wherein he went;*
*and his seed shall possess it.*

NUMBERS 14:24

# CHAPTER ONE

# What it Is for a Man to Follow God Fully

*T*he second doctrine follows: **It is the high praise of servants that they follow God fully.** This is their commendation: they have their hearts go fully in the ways of obedience to fulfill the good will of the Lord. This is that perfect heart which God so often calls for in Scripture, and for which so many of God's servants are commended in the Word. Genesis 17:1: "Walk before me," said God to Abra-ham, "and be thou perfect." Deuteronomy 18:13: "Thou shalt be perfect with the Lord thy God." This Noah is commended for in Genesis 6:9. He was a just man, and perfect in his generations. So Job 1:1. He was perfect and upright. The want of this was the stain and blot of Solomon (1 Kings 11:6). The text there says he went not fully after the Lord as did David his father. This likewise was the stain of the Church of Sardis in Revelation 3:2: "I have not found thy ways perfect." The words are, "I have not found thy ways filled up." You have not filled up your course in following Me. Something indeed you have done, but you have not followed Me fully. To have a heart full of goodness, as Saint Paul testifies of the Romans 15:14, and to have a life full of good works, as is witnessed of Tabitha in Acts 9:36, is the excellency of a godly man. This is the true declaration of the excellency of that spirit wherein this glory consists.

In this first chapter we shall first show what it is to follow God fully, or what the frame of the spirit is in following the Lord fully. In the second chapter, we shall show wherein the true excellency of this lies. In the remaining chapters we shall apply it.

Take this caution: when we speak of a fullness in following the Lord, we do not mean a legal fullness, such as fullness wherein there is no want or imperfection. Not to sin is here only our law; in heaven it shall be our reward. But there is a true following the Lord fully that is attained even in this life, an evangelical fullness, and that is the fullness that we are to speak of.

The gospel requires perfection as well as the law, though in a different manner:

There is a fullness of all graces. Though not the degree of all graces, yet the truth of every grace. There is no grace wanting where this evangelical fullness is.

There is no want, no, not of any degree, wherein the soul rests. There is such a perfection as the soul takes no liberty to itself to fail in anything.

There are sincere aims, as in the sight of God, to attain to the highest perfection, the full measure of holiness.

There is that uprightness of the soul such that it not only desires and endeavors to attain, but indeed attains to the truth of what I shall deliver.

First, the heart is fully set and resolved for God. There is fullness of resolution. So the Septuagint translates Joshua 14:8, where Caleb speaks of his following God fully: "I decreed, I determined to follow Him." The heart is fully taken off from shiftings, from hankerings after other things, from the engagements that before it had—from disputings, reasonings for the ways of the flesh. It does not hang between two things as unsettled, unresolved, or wavering, but is truly and fully taken off, and the resolutions are fully set upon the ways of God. Many have some convictions, some stirrings, some makings towards the ways of God, some approbation of them. They think, "It would be well if we could do this." Surely they are the best men who can do thus; but still some engagement holds them fast. They have thoughts flitting up and down; they would and they would not; they could like it well were it not for this thing; this inconvenience and the other trouble would follow. And so they delay and put off and think.

It may be they may hereafter do better. Their good desires and inclinations, they hope, may serve for the present. And thus they stand baffling with God and their own souls. They are, as Seneca says of some, always about to live. But the soul who fully follows God is fully broken off from former ways. Its thoughts come to a determinate issue. It is resolved against them whatsoever becomes of it, resolved to listen no more to reasonings of flesh and blood. Paul says of himself in Galatians 1:15–16 that after it pleased God to call him by His grace and to reveal His Son in him, immediately he conferred not with flesh and blood.

Many are a great while before they are this fully taken off. They are as Agrippa in Acts 26:28, *almost* persuaded to become Christians. The truths of God move them, but do not thoroughly persuade them. They strive with them, but do not thoroughly vanquish them. The Spirit of God leaves some in the very birth, that there is never strength to bring forth; but it is a most blessed thing when the heart comes off kindly and fully. Now it is not so ready to raise objections against the ways of God, nor to hearken to objections raised by others, as it was before. When the fire is fully kindled, there is little smoke. At first the smoke rises thick so that we can see no fire. The reason of so many arguings and objections of the flesh is that the heart is not fully taken off. Tertullian has a notable expression to this purpose: "How wise an arguer does the pride of man seem to itself when it is afraid to lose some worldly joys!" It is the engagement of man's heart to his lust that makes him think there is any strength in those objections and reasonings that he has in his heart against God's ways. When the heart is taken off these things, they vanish of themselves.

Second, there is a fullness of all the faculties of the soul working after God; full apprehensions, full affections; the soul is filled with the will of God. Colossians 4:12: "That ye may stand perfect, and full in all the will of God," as the sails are filled with the wind. "My soul and all that is within me praise the Lord," said David. As it is in giving men full possession of a house—they give up the keys of every room—so here the soul gives up every faculty to God. The whole soul opens itself to receive the Lord and His truth. There is a loving the Lord with all the mind, with all the heart, and with all the soul. There is a spiritual life quickening every faculty. There is a sanctification throughout every faculty, though no faculty is thoroughly sanctified.

Third, the soul follows God fully, with regard to its true endeavors, to put forth what strength it has in following the Lord. All the faculties work, and it is not satisfied that they should work remissly, but it would have them work fervently and powerfully as did David. Psalm 63:8: "My soul follows hard after Thee." There is a panting of the heart, a gasping of the spirit after the Lord; "As the hart panteth after the water brooks, so panteth my soul after Thee, O God," said David in Psalm 42:1. "My heart breaketh for the longing it hath unto Thy judgments" (Psalm 119:20). The spirit boils in fervor while it is serving the Lord. Romans 12:11: "Fervent in spirit, serving the Lord." Isaiah 26:9: "With my soul," said the prophet, "I have desired Thee, and with my spirit within me will I seek Thee." This soul not only loves God with all the mind and with all the heart, but with all the strength too. There is no strength reserved for anything else but the Lord.

Fourth, the soul that fully follows the Lord follows Him without delay in the use of all means. Delaying and putting off is an argument of remissness. David's soul followed hard after the Lord, as we noted before in the 63rd Psalm; and this made him seek the Lord early, verse 1: "O God, Thou art my God, early will I seek Thee," said he. The present time is the fullness of time with such a soul. We read that Haman, in Esther 3:5, was full of wrath; and hence he procured that the posts should be hastened about his work in destroying the Jews, verse 15. The godly soul sets upon all means, whatever way it may be brought near to God, either by ordinary means or by extraordinary. It uses all ordinances conscionably in their season, will abstain from all occasions of evil, and avoids all hindrances to that which is good. If this man knows anything may further him in bringing his heart nearer to God, he readily and thankfully embraces it and makes use of it. He uses all means, and yet does not rest in any means.

Fifth, the soul that follows God fully follows Him in all the ways of His commandments. The Lord said of David in Acts 13:22 that He had found a man who would fulfill all His will. In the original, the word is in the plural number, "who would fulfill all His wills." There are many reasons given why David was called "a man after God's own heart." Some think it was because he was such a broken-hearted man. Others say it was because he had such a thankful heart. But this Scripture resolves it for us, for God says that He had found a man after His own heart, and gives the reason that he would "fulfill all His wills." This soul desires to fulfill all righteousness, as Christ said of Himself in Matthew 3:15: "It became Him to fulfill all righteousness." It desires to yield obedience to God, and "to be holy in all manner of conversation," as the apostle says in 1 Peter 1:15. "Then shall not I be ashamed," said David, "when I have respect unto all Thy commandments" (Psalm 119:6).

We have a notable place for this universality of obedience in Colossians 1:10–11: "We pray that ye might be fulfilled in all knowledge of His will, in all wisdom, that ye might walk worthy of the Lord, and please Him in all things, being fruitful in all good works, strengthened with all might, through His glorious power, to all patience." There are six *alls* in this Scripture. A heart that is fully for God is for *all* God's ways in *all* things. It is not willing to balk at any of God's ways. Zechariah and Elizabeth were two choice spirits indeed, and this was their honor: they walked with God in all the commandments and in the ordinances of the Lord were blameless (Luke 1:6).

## What the Soul that Is Willing to Follow the Lord Fully Will Do

1. It is willing to follow the Lord in difficult duties, when it must put the flesh to it, in duties that require pains and much labor, that cannot be done without some hard things attending on them. God has some hard pieces of service to put His people upon to try the uprightness of their hearts, the sincerity and power of their love for Him. And God takes it exceedingly well when they will follow Him in such duties. He put Abraham upon a hard piece of service in offering his son. Yet Abraham was willing to follow Him in that. "Now," said He, "I know you love Me." It is nothing to follow God in such duties as will so

suit with us, wherein we need put ourselves to no trouble. Many are well content with such duties, and seem to yield to God in them; but go beyond those and put them upon further duties and they do not stir. The rusty hand of a sundial—if you come at that time of the day wherein the hour falls out the same as where the hand stands it seems to go right, but if you pass that time the hand stands still—goes no further than it did and so shows the dial not to be good. So here, when it falls out that a duty is enjoined which is suitable to a man's mind and ends, he will readily yield to it and seem as if he made conscience of obedience to God in it; but if you put him further in duties that are not so suitable to him, there he does not stir because of the difficulty which he sees in them. And in this he shows the falseness of his heart, that he does not follow God fully.

2. Again, one who follows God fully will follow him in discountenanced duty. Some duties are liked well enough in the world, for reason tells every man that God must have some service. Some general way of serving God all rational men approve of. And if God required a man to follow Him in no other duties but these it would be fine, but there are some others that will make Him to be observed; some ways in which he follows the Lord shall cause him to be reckoned among such kind of men of whose number he does not like to be counted as one. He knows they are discountenanced and despised, and this he cannot bear; and therefore those are duties he has no mind to, and then thinks to himself: "Why may not my obedience in other things serve the turn?"

3. Yet further, one who is willing to follow God fully in all duties will follow Him in those where he sees no reason but the bare command of God. It is enough to him that they are commanded of God. It is not for the Lord to give account of His ways to His creatures; it is enough for us that He bids

us follow Him. Absolute obedience is that which is our duty. There is always reason enough in God's will, but whether we see it or not, if we can but see the commandment it is enough for us. We take too much upon us to dispute about the reason of things with God. We must not be judges of the Law, but doers of it.

Saul could see no reason why he might not spare the best of the cattle, especially when he did it to keep them for sacrifice, but it cost him his kingdom. God rejected him for it and told him, "Obedience is better than sacrifice" (1 Samuel 15:22). Luther said that he would rather obey than work miracles. And Cassianus reports of one Johannes Abbas, who, when he was young, was willing for a whole year to fetch water every day, walking nearly two miles to water a dry stick, because he was commanded so to do. He thought it reason enough to do unreasonable things to show his obedience unto man whose will is many times unreasonable. How much more reason is there, then, that we should show our obedience to God in duties where, through our weakness, we cannot see the reason, when we may be sure that there is always reason enough if we were able to see it.

4. Yet further, the soul that is willing to follow God in all duties will follow Him in commandments that are accounted little commandments. God expects faithfulness in little things. God prizes every tittle of His Law more worthy than heaven and earth, however we may slight many things in it, and think them too small to put any great bond upon us. Christ said that heaven and earth would pass away, but not one jot or tittle of His Word. It is as if He said, "If heaven and earth were in one balance, and any jot and tittle of My Word in another, and if one of them must perish, I would rather that heaven should perish than that one jot or tittle of My Word should fail."

The authority of heaven puts weight on things that are never so little in themselves. If man's authority does this, how much more divine authority? Man cannot bear disobedience in little things, though the things are very small in themselves; yet if they are commanded by authority, it is justly expected that they should be regarded. Shall man's authority make small things to be accounted great, and shall God's authority do nothing? Obedience in small things is due to magistrates; much more is it due to God. "Give to Caesar the things that are Caesar's, and to God the things that are God's" (Matthew 22:21). It is observable in that place that the article is twice repeated in the Greek text when He speaks of God, more than when He speaks of Caesar, showing that our special care should be to give God His due.

5. Last, not to instance in any more particulars, the soul that follows God fully in all duties is willing to follow Him in duties wherein it must go alone. It is willing to follow God in solitary paths. Many men, if they might have company along the way in following the Lord, would be content; but to go all alone in such solitary ways wherein they can see none go before them, wherein they can have none along with them, where few or none are likely to follow after them, is tedious. But a child of God thinks he has enough in that he has God with him, that he walks along with God. This is company enough, let the way be what it will. As David said in Psalm 23:4: "Though I walk through the valley of the shadow of death, yet Thou art with me." God promises that He will go before His people; that is enough, though there be none else. It is true, company in God's ways is delightful, and it is a sad thing that there is so little a tract in God's paths. It was the complaint of God's people in Lamentations 1:4 that the ways of Zion mourned because none came in them. But if company cannot be had, it is enough that we have the Lord. 2 Timothy 4:16–17: "At my first answer," said Paul,

"no man stood with me, but all men forsook me; notwithstanding the Lord stood with me." Elijah thought he was left alone; he could see no man go the way he did. Yet he continued in his fervor and zeal, "following the Lord." Indeed, we should rather follow the Lord because we see so few follow Him. What? Shall He have none to follow Him? As Christ said to His disciples when many forsook Him, "Will you also forsake me?"

Thus you see by these several instances that we must follow God fully in difficult duties, in discountenanced duties, in duties wherein we can see no reason but a bare command, in duties that seem to be small, and in duties wherein if we follow God we must follow Him alone. The soul that follows God fully will follow Him in these, and so, by the same reasoning, in all other duties in which God shall require that we follow Him. And this is the precious, choice spirit we spoke of before, which shows itself in that it is willing to follow God fully.

You know, it is required of us to be perfect as God Himself is perfect, to be holy as God is holy. Yea, this the gospel requires of us. But how can that be? In this: God's perfection and holiness are made known to us in His will, in His commandments. Now, however largely they are set forth to us in these, so large must our obedience be. Though we cannot attain to the *degree*, yet our hearts must enlarge themselves to the *things*, to whatever part of God's will God makes known His perfection and holiness by. "Thy commandment is very broad," said David in Psalm 119:96, yet godliness enlarges the heart to every duty it calls for. There is a grace within the soul suitable to every duty the Law requires.

"It may be this is indeed," some may think, "in those who are eminent in grace, upon whom God has bestowed a great measure of His Spirit; but is this in everyone that has any truth?"

Wherefore, for answer, let us know there is this perfection

or else there is no truth at all. Remember, I do not speak now of the perfection of degrees. In this consists the right straightness of a man's heart. A straight line will touch with another straight line in every point. But a crooked line will not; it touches only here and there in some points. So straight hearts will join with God's law in every part, but crooked and perverse hearts only in some, only so far as may serve their own turns. In this consists the true plainness of a man's spirit. As plain things will join likewise in every point one with another, but round and rugged things will not, so proud, swollen hearts and rugged spirits will not close fully with God's truths. But where there is plainness of spirit, there is a full closing, a thorough union.

There is a dangerous mistake about this point that yet is a common mistake; multitudes of people miscarry everlastingly upon this mistake. They think that because we cannot in this life attain to the perfection of holiness in degree, therefore no perfection at all is necessary, but they may be saved without it. They think, therefore, that if they do some good things, if they obey some commandments, it is sufficient, though they take liberty to themselves in other things. They find they can yield in some things, yet other things of God's will are exceedingly unsuitable to them. Be convinced of your mistake herein: a godly man indeed is weak and cannot attain to the performance of every part of God's will, but the frame of his heart is to every part. Every part is suitable to his spirit. He esteems all the precepts of God concerning all things to be right, and he hates every false way. He finds the Law of God, in the latitude of it, written in his heart. There is no command of God that is not dearer to him than all the world. Mark that place in Job 8:20: "God will not cast away the perfect man, neither will He help the evildoers." The perfect man is opposed to the evildoers who shall be cast away. If you are not perfect in this sense that has been spoken of, then you are an evildoer who must be cast away, however glorious many of your actions may seem to be.

Ezekiel 18:21 is usually taken for the place of the greatest mercy in all the Scripture, and by many is exceedingly abused. Yet see what that verse requires of men in their repentance. The words are usually quoted like this: "At what time soever a sinner repents of his sin, I will blot out his iniquities, saith the Lord." Those words are not in any place of Scripture, but there are words close to those in this place in Ezekiel. And in no other place is God's mercy to a sinner more fully revealed. There is no text in Scripture that comes nearer to that which men ordinarily say than this verse, and the 27th and 28th verses in the same chapter, and see how God's mind is made known there. The words of the Scripture are thus: "If the wicked will turn from all his sins that he hath committed, and *keep all My statutes*, and do that which is lawful and right, he shall surely live." And verse 28: "Because he considereth, and *turns from all his transgressions*." Thus you see that God, in the largest promises of His mercy to those who have the least measure of grace, requires turning from all sins and keeping all His statutes. And this God states to show the infinite equity of His way towards sinners. As if he should say, "Unless this is done, there is no man's conscience in the world but must acknowledge it to be infinitely just and equitable that he should perish everlastingly. If there is any way of wickedness reserved, if any statute of Mine is neglected, if he thinks to have mercy without a universal turning from his sin, without a universal obedience, his conscience will tell him that it is an inequitable and unreasonable thing that he should ever expect it."

And yet further, because you think that this universality of obedience should be expected only from some who are eminent in grace, who have attained to a great measure of godliness, consider what is required of poor widows. 1 Timothy 5:10: "They must diligently follow every good work."

First, they must not only have good desires, but good works.

Second, they must follow good works.

Third, they must diligently follow them.

Fourth, they must diligently follow *every* good work.

Fifth, they must so follow as they must be well reported of for it.

Yea, sixth, they must do all this or else they must not be received into the Church.

Surely, then, it is a shame for any man, especially of parts and abilities, to plead weakness when so much is required of poor women. Certainly it is not weakness, but falseness of heart that is contrary to universality of obedience, to following the Lord fully in this respect. The vessel of honor is distinguished from the vessel of dishonor in 2 Timothy 2:21 by this characteristic: it is one that is sanctified and prepared for every good work. You know what James 1:26 says: "If any man seems to be religious and bridles not his tongue, but deceives his own heart, this man's religion is in vain." It is a heavy censure that all a man's religion is in vain for one fault, and that but for a fault in the tongue. Yet this is the censure of the Holy Ghost. No question, such men who were guilty herein would reason thus with themselves: "We cannot be perfect in this life; we perform many duties of religion; and therefore we hope, though we fail in this one thing, that we shall do well enough. God will accept us."

No, said James. He deceives his own heart. Such a one shall never be accepted. To the like effect is that question of our Savior in John 5:44: "How can ye believe on Me, which receive honor one of another?" This was enough to keep them off forever from Christ; and yet this was but an inward sin, no outward, gross, crying sin in the esteem of the world. Let a man be never so glorious in never so many duties of religion, yet, certainly, giving liberty to himself in any one lust is enough to keep him off forever from God, from partaking of good in Him.

If a wife is never so obliging to her husband, yielding to him in never so many things, seeking to give him contentment in his desires in never so many ways, yet if she entertains any other lover besides him it is enough to alienate his spirit from her forever.

What God says to Solomon in 1 Kings 9:4 is very observable for our purpose. After Solomon had finished that glorious temple for the honor of the Lord, after he had assembled all the elders of Israel, all the heads of the tribes, the chief of the fathers of the children of Israel, to bring up the Ark of the Lord with all solemnity to the temple he had made for it, after he had made such an excellent prayer before all the people, when that was done, that he might show his further respect unto the Lord, he offered to the Lord two and twenty thousand oxen, and one hundred and twenty thousand sheep. And in his rejoicing in this great work, he made a great feast with the people for seven days; and to those he added seven days more, and sent away the people with joyful and glad hearts. And here were great things done in honor to God. Yet all this would not serve Solomon's turn. But in 9:4, after all this, God said to him, "If thou wilt walk before Me, as David thy father walked, in integrity of heart and uprightness, to do according to all that I have commanded thee, then I will establish the throne of thy kingdom."

It is as if He should have said, "Do not think to put Me off with anything you have done. Though the things are great things, yet I expect walking according to all that I have commanded you or else all is nothing." Therefore, as before we noted, he was charged by God in 11:6 that he did not go fully after the Lord.

One would have thought those glorious actions that he did would have been enough to have gotten him the commendation of going fully after God. But we see it would not be. There must be, besides these, a walking according to all that God commands, keeping His statutes and His judgments. Yea, and it is observable in 9:6–7, where God said after all this, "If you shall at all turn from following Me, you, or your children . . . then will I cut off Israel." We must take heed of the least failing in our following the Lord. God threatened Solomon after he had done so much that if he at all turned from following Him, He would cut him off.

It is not our forwardness in some good things, it is not our serviceableness in some public and worthy employments that will serve our turns if we do not make conscience of every duty, of secret duties, and of every duty constantly. God has so connected the duties of His Law one to another that if there is not a conscionable care to walk according to all, it is accounted as the breach of all according to James 2:10: "Whosoever shall keep the whole Law, and yet offend in one point, is guilty of all." The bond of all is broken; the authority of all is slighted; and that evil disposition that causes man to venture upon the breach of one is such that if the breach of others might serve for his own ends as well as that one, it would make him venture upon the breach of any.

To draw to a conclusion of this argument, let us know that if the heart is right, it is willing to be cast into the mold of the Word to receive whatever print the Word will put upon it, to be in whatever form the Word will have it. Metals that are cast into a mold receive the print of the mold, print for print in every part; and this is the heart that indeed follows God fully. This is Paul's expression in Romans 6:17: "You have obeyed from the heart that form of doctrine unto which you were delivered." So the words are in the original. The form of doctrine is compared to the mold, and those who sincerely obey from the heart are compared to the metal delivered into this mold that takes impression from it, in one part as well as in another. No sincere obedience from the heart means no true following of God fully without this. I have been so long in this particular because the mistake is so widespread and dangerous.

Then does the heart fully follow after the Lord, when it is indeed willing to search fully into every truth that it does not fully know, with a readiness to lie under the power of it. Such a man is not afraid of any truth of God, lest it should put him upon that he has no mind to. Ahab was afraid to inquire of Micaiah what the mind of God was because he never prophesied good unto him; but the man who follows the Lord fully always accounts the word of the Lord to be good to him. Micah 2:7: "Do not my words do good to him that walks uprightly?" He says to the Lord, as Elihu did in Job 34:32, "That which I see not, teach thou me: if I have done iniquity, I will do no more." Lord, that which I know not, teach me; and wherein I have failed, I shall conscionably endeavor to reform. Oh, let the Word of God be glorified forever, whatsoever becomes of me! Let it come in the full latitude of it, my soul shall yield to it. My heart is prepared to submit to whatsoever truth God shall make known to me."

I remember in one of the epistles written to Oecolampadius a notable expression of one Baldassar, a minister in Germany, writing to him: "Let the word of the Lord come, let it come, and we will submit to it, if we had many hundred necks to put under." This is yet a degree further; for there are many who dare not go against known truths for their conscience would fly in their faces, but there are some truths which they are afraid to know, which they are secretly willing to put off, lest they should come to know them. And this is an argument that their hearts are not fully after the Lord: when men are not convinced of many truths, not because there is not light enough to convince them, but because they are not willing to be convinced. They strive to keep out the power of the truth from their hearts. They are not willing that such unsuitable truths should come into their judgments. They seek to shift them off. When the truth stands and pleads for entrance, they seek one shift or another to put it off withal. Hebrews 12:25: "See that ye refuse not Him that speaketh." The words are: "See that ye shift not Him off that speaketh." In the meaning of that word, as it is in the original, we have this much signified to us: Christ in His truths comes to ask entrance, and we must take heed that we do not put Him off. And if the truth has gotten into our judgment, we must take heed we do not strive to get conscience off from it; and if conscience has closed with it, we must take heed we strive not to get it out of conscience again, and then think it a sufficient plea to satisfy ourselves and others in the actions we do that now our judgments are better informed. The truth indeed is that our lusts are more satisfied and the corruptions of our hearts are more increased. Oh, take heed forever of laboring to blind our understandings, of withholding the truth in unrighteousness, of imprisoning it to keep it from working with power upon our hearts! This distemper of heart is exceedingly opposite to following the Lord fully.

To follow God fully is to follow Him so as to be willing to venture the loss of all for Him, willing to decline and cast off whatever comes in the way, though never so dear unto us; to follow Him close, whatever comes in competition with Him— when we cannot follow Him without parting with much for Him, when our following Him will cost us the loss of our formerly most dear comforts and contentments; to follow the Lamb wherever He goes, through all afflictions, through all straits, knowing that this way, though it is a way of blood, yet leads to the throne.

6. To follow Christ is to go to Mount Calvary where He is to suffer as well as to that mount that we read of in Isaiah 25:6 where the Lord makes His people "a feast of fat things, a feast of wines, a feast of fat things full of marrow." It is nothing to follow Him when our comforts, peace, ease, and honor go along together with Him. It cannot then be known whether we follow Him or not, or whether it is our own ends that we follow.

When a servingman follows two gentlemen, we know not which of these two he follows till they part. Then you shall see which was his master. So when Christ and our own ends part one from another, then is the trial of which was followed before. We must love the truth not only when we can live upon it, when we can get advantage by it, but also when it must live upon us, when it must have our estates, our peace, our names, our liberties, our lives to live upon, and to maintained by. We must follow Him when it means that we must deny ourselves and take up our cross, when we must thoroughly deny ourselves; for the word in the original is a compound, noting more than a single, more than an ordinary self-denial. We must take up our cross and not choose what cross we are willing to meet with, to think, "If it were such an affliction that such a man had, I could bear it; but I know not how to bear this." But it must be our cross, and we must willingly take it up, and that daily too.

We must be willing to follow Him through the wilderness. Song of Solomon 8:5: "Who is this that cometh from the wilderness, leaning on her beloved?" The wilderness is the troubles and afflictions of the Church. She comes through them with her Beloved, resting herself upon Him. If the Lord will lead us through the fire and through the water, we must follow Him there. If He will lead us where fiery serpents and scorpions are, we must follow Him there (Deuteronomy 8:15). Josephus, writing of the times of Christ, said, "There was one Jesus, a wise man in those times, if it be lawful to call Him a man, for He did divers admirable works, yet He was condemned to the cross; but notwithstanding this, those who followed Him from the beginning did not forbear to love Him because of the ignominy of His death, but followed Him still."

To follow a crucified Christ, a condemned Christ, to follow Him in the bloody paths of His sufferings, is to follow Him fully indeed. When one came and told Christ that he would follow Him wherever He went (Matthew 8:19), Jesus said unto him, "The foxes have holes, and the birds of the air have nests, but the Son of Man hath not whereon to lay his head." It is as if He had said, "You must not expect great matter in following Me, but you must be content to suffer hard things." Christ told the young man who came running to Him to know what he should do for eternal life that if he would be perfect, he must sell all and then come and follow Him. If he would follow Him fully, he must be content to part with all for Christ, to sell all, as the wise merchant sold all for the pearl. "If there be anything in the world that you are not willing to part with, if anything that you are not willing to suffer, you cannot follow Me fully." In this consists the uprightness of heart, to go in a right line to God, whatever comes between God and us; not to fetch a compass, but to go through it, for if we fetch a compass, the line is not right. We must therefore strike through all troubles and hazards we meet with, still keep our way, not break the hedge of any commandment to avoid any piece of foul way.

Many *think* they desire to follow God, but when they meet with some trouble in their way they seek to go around it, and yet

hope to come to God well enough at last. They would be loath
*not* to be accounted followers of God. But let such know that
what they think to be their wisdom is a declining from uprightness. Many follow God as the dog follows his master. When he
comes by a piece of meat he then lets his master go and turns
aside to it. Many seem to be forward in their profession of religion till they meet with some opportunity of satisfying their
lusts; then they leave off and turn aside to the enjoyment of
them. But the heart that fully follows God is not only willing
to part with any lust for Christ, it gives up itself to God so that
whatever becomes of his estate, credit, liberty, comforts, life, it
is agreeable to him if that is what God pleases. It is not solicitous about these things. The business it has to do is to follow
the Lord. It knows that it is the work of the Lord to take care for
it about these things while it is following Him.

It is said of Amaziah in 2 Chronicles 25:2 that "he did that
indeed which was right in the sight of the Lord, but not with a
perfect heart." He did many good things, but he did not have a
heart to follow God fully. And this was one argument of it, verse
9, that he was so solicitous about his money. For when the man
of God came to him and told him the mind of God, that he
must not have the army of Israel to go with him because he had
hired the army with a hundred talents, he was very solicitous
what he should do for his money. For so he said, "But what shall
we do for the hundred talents which I have given to the army
of Israel?" If his heart had been right and full in following God
as it should have been, it would have been enough for him to
have known the command of God, let become of the hundred
talents what will.

7. To follow God fully is to follow Him only, so as to be willing to dedicate and devote whatever God lets us still enjoy to
God alone. If we have any gifts, any estate, any esteem in the

world, all shall be employed for God alone, all shall be laid out for Him.

As we must be willing to lose all things for Him when He calls for them, so we must endeavor to use all things for Him while we enjoy them. To follow God fully is to follow Him as the highest good, as the only good, as the all-sufficient good, as the fountain of all good, as the rule of all good, to follow Him so as to follow nothing else but God. We are not only to follow God chiefly, that is, more than to follow anything else, but we must follow Him only.

But how is that?

We must follow God in our following anything else. We must follow all for God, in reference to God, in subordination under God, and then we cannot be said to follow the creature, but it is God that is followed in it. When God is followed in reference and subordination to any good in the creature, it is not then God but the creature that we follow; so when the creature is followed in subordination to God, it is God and not the creature that is followed. When David was in the dry wilderness, no question he desired water. Yet Psalm 63:1 says, "I thirst after Thee, O Lord, in a dry and barren wilderness, where no water is." He does not say, "I thirst after water," but "after Thee," because he sought all in reference to God. And so it was God alone that he thirsted for. When we desire nothing, when we seek after nothing, when we let out our hearts to nothing, use or enjoy nothing but in order to God; when all the good, comfort, sweetness, and desirableness in any creature are in the reference they have to God—so far as God is in it, as God is honored or enjoyed by it—when God alone is lifted up in the heart in the use of every creature, this is to follow God fully. "Thou shalt worship the Lord thy God, and Him only shalt thou serve." You shall follow the Lord your God, and Him only shall you follow.

Christ charged the Jews, in John 5:44, that they did not seek the honor that came from God only; and this was that which kept them from believing. This is enough to keep us off from God forever.

If we would have our heart come up fully to God only, it is not enough to seek the honor that comes from God; we must seek the honor that comes from God only. And this is the true singleness of heart that the Scripture speaks of when it singles out this object and eyes it alone.

The doubleness of a man's heart consists not so much in that it is otherwise within than what it appears outwardly, but in that it is divided to diverse objects. It does not fix upon God as the only object. As double-minded men have double objects, so they have double motions. They are as the planets that are carried in their motion one way by the heavens, but have besides a private motion of their own. Many are carried to God by some external, yea, it may be, internal motives; but they have a private motion of their own in another way to other things. God alone is not the center of their hearts.

8. The soul then follows God fully when it carries through the work it undertakes against all discouragements and hindrances. Like a ship coming with full sail, it bears down before it. It not only works, but works thoroughly; it works out what it does. Philippians 2:12: "Work out your salvation." Work till you get the work done. This soul works after God in His ways, and that with power. Though it finds no good comes in by them for the present, though it has worked a long time and yet sees nothing coming in, it murmurs not; it repines not; it repents not of anything it has done for God. It does not complain with those hypocrites in Isaiah 58:3: "Wherefore have we fasted, and Thou seest not, and wherefore have we afflicted our souls, and Thou regardest not?" Nor with those in Malachi 1:13 who say,

"What a weariness is this!" and those in 3:14 who say, "It is in vain to serve the Lord, and what profit is there that we have kept His ordinances, and that we have walked mournfully before the Lord of Hosts?"

But the soul that follows God fully makes no such complaints but goes on still in the way of God. Though the flesh is weary and tired, it goes on still. Though Gideon and the three hundred men who were with him (Judges 8:4), were faint, yet they went on pursuing. So here, though there may be much faintness and weakness, yet the soul does not think of turning back again, but goes on still pursuing in the way it has begun. It is glad it has done anything for God, and it resolves still to do more however God pleases to deal with it. Though he may be weary *in* his following the Lord, yet he is not weary *of* following the Lord.

Many follow the Lord as a beggar follows a man: only in expectation of alms. He follows him a furlong or two, begging; but if he sees the man go still from him, he leaves off and lets him go. So many will pray and hear and seek after God for a while; but if they do not get what they expected, they grow weary and leave off. Duties that bring present comfort with them, many can be content to be exercised in; but if they find nothing coming in by them their hearts sink in discouragement; they have no heart to do anything.

It is said of Ephraim in Hosea 10:11: "Ephraim is as a heifer that loves to tread out the corn." Ephraim loved to tread out the corn but not to plow. While the heifer was treading out the corn it fed upon the corn, and so had present delight in the work it did. But the heifer that plowed labored and spent its strength, but had no refreshment till after the work was done. Thus it is with many who work, who have present joy, who have present refreshment in it: while they are about it they can take contentment in it; but if they must work and tire the flesh, and yet have not present refreshing but must continue working a great while and stay till the accomplishment of the work before any benefit comes by it, they do not like it. But one who follows the Lord fully resolves to follow Him though He hides himself. Psalm 101:2: "I will behave myself wisely, in a perfect way; oh, when wilt Thou come unto me? I will walk within my house with a perfect heart." As if David had said, "I am resolved to walk before Thee in a perfect way, and yet I have not Thy gracious presence with me. Oh, when wilt Thou come unto me? But whatever becomes of me, I am determined to continue walking within my house with a perfect heart."

The like place we have in Psalm 119:8: "I will keep Thy statutes; oh, forsake me not utterly." As if he had said, "O Lord, Thou hast in some degree forsaken me, Thou seemest as if Thou wouldest forsake me; yet, Lord, I am determined that I will keep Thy statutes."

Thus the upright heart resolves: "Though I should perish everlastingly, yet I will perish following the Lord; and if I cannot follow Him, I will cry after Him: and if I cannot cry after Him, I will look towards Him; yea, though He appear to be angry, yet will I follow Him." Job said, "Though he kills me, yet will I trust in Him." Though there is much guiltiness upon the spirit, so that the devil and an unbelieving, sullen heart would much discourage it from following after the Lord, yet still it will not leave off, but labors to encourage itself as Samuel did the people. 1 Samuel 12:20–21: "Samuel said unto the people, 'Fear not; ye have done all this wickedness, yet turn not aside from following the Lord, but serve the Lord with all your heart, and turn you not aside: for then should you go after vain things, which cannot profit nor deliver, for they are vain.' "

Thus the soul that follows the Lord reasons with itself: "Though it is true I have sinned and my iniquities are great,

that God may justly be provoked and forever reject me, yet I will
not turn aside from following Him. I know there is no good to
be gotten elsewhere. Though I am unworthy of mercy, yet God
is worthy of honor, and therefore, whatever I can do I will, that
God may have honor though I perish."

Yea, though this soul receives many repulses, still it will follow. Though Christ called the woman of Canaan a dog, yet she
did not leave. She acknowledged herself to be a dog, yet still
she sought Him. Yea, though God seems to go in cross ways,
quite contrary to what the soul expected, yet still this soul will
follow Him even in those ways. The Lord called Abraham to
follow Him into a land that would flow with milk and honey
(Genesis 12:1). Abraham was content to leave his own country,
his father's house, his kindred, and all his friends; and notwithstanding, as soon as he came into that land, he found there was
a famine in the land, verse 10. He was forced to get into Egypt,
and that with the peril of his life, or else he would have starved.
Flesh and blood would have murmured greatly at this and said,
"What? Is this the land that God said He would show me? Is this
the fruitful land for which I must leave my country and all my
friends? Now as soon as I come into it, I am ready to starve in
it!" Yet Abraham followed God in all the ways He was pleased
to lead him in. When God promised to multiply his seed as the
stars of heaven, yet for twenty years after this Sarah was barren.
God seemed to neglect His promise. And after he had a child
in whom all the nations of the earth were to be blessed, yet this
child Abraham must kill. Here God seemed to go cross to His
promise, yet Abraham followed God fully indeed. He looked
up to the goodness of God in Himself and in His promise, not
as it appeared to sense. He saw more good in the promise than
in all the things in the world though he saw nothing, though he
felt nothing in himself nor in any creature present.

Whatever work the godly soul follows the Lord in, he will not leave imperfect. He will not give over till he sees something come of it. If he follows God for a broken heart, he will pray and meditate, and pray and meditate again, a thousand times, and a thousand times again, till the work comes to some effect. So it is for power over a corruption and strength in any grace: where there is truth of grace, there will be working like fire that never stops working till it breaks forth and gets the victory.

Hence I refer you to that place of our Savior (Matthew 12:20), where He said He will not quench the smoking flax nor break the bruised reed till He sends forth judgment into victory. If we observe the place of the prophet from whence this is taken (Isaiah 42:3), the words are: "He shall bring forth judgment unto truth," noting that wherever there is truth there will be victory. Christ will nourish the smoking flax, that is, the least work of grace, till judgment, that is, till this work of sanctification is brought into victory and overcomes what opposes it. If he brings any beginnings of grace to truth, the victory is already gotten.

It is reported that Mister Bradford would never leave off when he was in holy duties till he found something coming in; in confession of sin, till he found his heart melt and break for sin; in seeking pardon, till he found some quieting of his spirit, in some intimation from God of His love; in grace, till he found his heart warmed and quickened. It is an excellent thing indeed to resolve to follow the Lord in duty, though nothing should come by it to ourselves. But the heart that is right will never be satisfied in the performance of a duty till it finds some manifestation of God's presence in it, some work of God put forth upon the heart by it. It will not rest in duty performed; it is not satisfied in good inclinations, in good desires it has, nor in gifts it receives; not in comforts it finds in the creature, nor in enlargements and more inward joys, but it must have grace and God; it must have some impression of God upon it to carry with it as a seal of that presence of God it enjoyed in the duty. It so strives with the Lord that it resolves not to let Him go till it gets a blessing.

It is a very full expression that Bernard had to this purpose in a few words. Oh, what a mercy it would be to continually enjoy what he said! "O Lord, I never go away from Thee without Thee." He means that he never left off duty till he got the presence of God, and so carried the Lord along with him. Oh, how often do we go from God without God! We think it enough that we have been before Him in holy duties, though indeed we still abide as strangers to Him, and He to us. How often does God send us empty away from His presence, which we should account a sore and grievous affliction? But here is the misery: we are not sensible of this; if we have our desires in the creature we are quieted and satisfied. Whereas, if our hearts were fully after the Lord as they ought, when we are before Him, we would cry to Him, as Moses did in another case, Exodus 33:15: "Except Thy presence go with me, Lord send me not hence."

9. One who follows God fully is willing to engage and bind himself to God by the most full and strong bonds and engagements that can be. His spirit is at the greatest liberty when he is most strongly bound to the Lord. 2 Chronicles 15:12 is very observable for this. Asa and his people entered into a covenant to seek the Lord God of their fathers with all their heart and with all their soul; yet so as whoever would not seek the Lord God should be put to death, whether small or great, man or woman. And they swore unto the Lord with shoutings, with trumpets, and with cornets. But were they not afterwards troubled that they had tied and bound themselves? Would they not have thought it better to have been at more liberty? No, surely,

for verse 15 says that "all Judah rejoiced in the oath." And the reason is given: "Because they had sworn with all their heart, and sought him with their whole soul." When any seek God with their whole heart, with their whole soul, they are not only willing to engage themselves to God, but they rejoice in their engagements. This Nehemiah, whose heart was fully set for God, did himself, and got the princes, the priests, Levites, and people to make a sure covenant, to write it, to seal it, chapter 9:38. And as if this were not engagement enough, they further entered into a curse and into an oath to walk in God's Law, to observe and do all the commandments of the Lord, and His judgments, and His statutes. Thus David discovered the fullness of his spirit in following after the Lord in that he not only promised but swore he would keep the righteous judgments of the Lord, Psalm 119:106. It is a sign that men's hearts are not fully taken off from their sin when they do not fully come off in the covenant of the Lord.

No, some may say, it is because we often covenant with God, and find we are overcome again, and break covenant with Him. And therefore we are afraid to enter into covenant any more. Is it not better not to covenant than not to perform?

I answer, it is true, if men covenant and willfully neglect, they would be better not to covenant at all. But when we enter into covenant, we have the testimony of our consciences that we labor as in the sight of God to fulfill our covenants that we make, and it is the burden of our souls that we fail in them. Then I say that we are still to go on and engage ourselves further. Our covenants do not aggravate our sin, but in time they will help us against our sin. This is one way that God has appointed to strengthen us; and therefore we must not complain of weakness and yet neglect any way appointed by God to get strength by.

10. To follow God fully is to abide in all these constantly to the end of our days. That is, we must be constant in God's ways. We must not think it enough to enter into them by fits and starts, but the ways of God must be our ordinary track. Proverbs 16:17: "The highway of the upright is to depart from evil." It is his common road and constant course, and we must continue faithful before the Lord unto death. It is the commendation of Hezekiah in 2 Kings 18:6, "He cleaved unto the Lord and departed not." And David, in Psalm 119:112, said, "He hath inclined his heart to perform God's statutes always." But as if that expression were not enough to signify his continuance, he added, "even unto the end." Job 17:9: "The righteous holds on his way." A heart that has given up itself fully to God never forsakes Him. There is no apostate in the world but if we could trace him along in his ways to his very beginning, we might find that in the entrance of his profession there was not a full giving up of himself to God. There was not an absolute surrender made of all that he was and had unto the Lord. It may be said of him, as it was of Amaziah, "Though he did that which was right in the sight of the Lord, yet he did it not with a perfect heart."

There are three reasons why it must be that the man who follows God fully must follow Him constantly and forever.

First, because wherever the Lord brings any to follow Him fully, He causes such a perfect breach between sin and the soul that there is no possibility that there should ever be a reconciliation made, that the breach should be made up again. An unsound heart so falls out with his sin that there remains a possibility of reconciliation; and therefore, when such a one finds trouble in God's service, he is willing to enter into parley again upon terms of agreement with his sin. But it is not so with a truly godly heart. There is such a breach made that there is no hope of reconciliation. It was Ahithophel's policy to get

Absalom to stick to him and never leave him to take away the fear he might still have, lest Absalom in time might be reconciled to his father and so leave him. Therefore he sought to make such a breach between him and his father so that there would never be any hope of reconciliation. And so that Absalom might be the surer to remain faithful to him, and the people that joined with him, he therefore advised that Absalom should go into his father's concubines upon the housetop in the sight of all the people (2 Samuel 16:21–22).

It is the wisdom of God that He may have followers never to leave Him, to make such breaches between sin and their souls at first so as there may never be hope of peace between them again. When the devil would draw one to be his forever, he seeks to make great breaches between God and him, so that if he should have ever any thoughts of returning, he may become discouraged and sink his spirit with thoughts of despair. He tells him there is no hope of good in returning that way, and therefore it would be better for him to continue as he is. Jeremiah 2:25: "Thou saidst, there is no hope; no, for I have loved strangers, and after them will I go." When the devil gets one who has been forward in the profession of religion to apostatize, he labors to make such a breach between him and his former course that the apostate not only falls off from it, but hates it, persecutes it, and turns deadly enemy to it. Then both the devil and wicked men think they are sure of him forever. Indeed, it is very seldom that ever such a one returns.

Bishop Latimer, in a sermon before King Edward, told of one who fell away from the known truth, and later fell to mocking and scorning it and yet was later touched in conscience for it. Beware of this sin, said Latimer, for I have known no more but this one man that ever fell from the truth, and afterwards repented. I have known many fall, but never any but this repent.

Now the breach between sin and the soul in conversion is as great as between God and the soul in apostasy. Yea, it is greater, for there is a possibility of reconciliation in the one, but never in the other. And therefore, as the one, because of this great breach between God and his soul, follows the devil and his destruction forever, so the other, because of the breach between sin and the soul, follows the Lord and His salvation forever. As in the one, the gifts of God's Spirit are so cast out as usually never to return again, so in the other, the unclean spirit is so cast out as to never come back again.

A second reason why the man who follows the Lord fully must follow Him forever is that, at the first giving up of himself to God, he was content to let go all other holds and all other hopes in all creature comforts whatever, and so to venture himself upon God as to be content to be miserable forever if he finds not enough in God to make him happy. He has so let all other things go that, if he should fail here, he has nowhere to retire. He has reserved no way, no means to help himself by if he should miscarry here. He has laid all the weight of all his comforts, of all his hopes, of all his happiness upon the Lord. He has no other prop that he does or can expect any support by. There is a blessed necessity upon him to follow the Lord forever, and this necessity the soul is glad of. This is the reason why God, in first bringing a soul home to Himself, uses so many means to take it off from all other things, namely, that it might follow Him forever.

It is reported of William the Conqueror that, when he came to invade England and had landed his soldiers, he sent back his ships that they might have no hope of retreating again, and so they were put upon a necessity of fighting it out to the utmost. Thus the Lord takes off the soul from all its former hopes and props that it may have no lingerings after anything but Himself, but thoroughly fight the good fight of faith, and with resolution hold on its course to the end.

But it is otherwise with a false, unsound heart. Though such a one may follow God in many glorious performances, yet it secretly reserves something in case of failing here. When it enters upon God's ways, it is enlightened so far as it thinks some good may be had here. Yea, it has a taste, it may be, of much sweetness in these ways, but dares not venture all upon them. He would be glad to have something to retire to in case he should fail here. He reserves a back door that he might turn another way, if this way should prove troublesome and dangerous. He enters upon God's ways not without suspicions and jealousies, that possibly he may meet with such inconveniences as may make him wish he had been more wise and not put himself in too far. He sees many others who have been deeply engaged and gone on so far in those ways wherein they meet with much trouble, many sore and heavy afflictions. He thinks they do, or at least may repent themselves, and wish they had not ventured themselves so far that now they know not how to go back again. And if they were to begin again, he thinks they would be wiser and hearken to grave advice that they proceed with more moderation.

The king of Navarre told Beza that he would launch no further into the sea than he might be sure to return safely unto the haven. Though he showed some countenance to religion, yet he would be sure to save himself. Many think it wisdom not to venture all in one place. It was once the speech of a deep politician that it was good to follow the truth, but not to follow it too near at the heels lest it dashed out his brains. Ananias and Sapphira would be Christians. They would join with the apostles, and saw that great things were done by them. Their possessions must be sold, and the money laid at the apostles' feet. But something must be reserved in case they should want later and repent that they had gone so far when it would be too late. And this is the very root of apostasy. But it is otherwise with a sincere heart that follows God fully. In such a one there is a holy kind of desperateness so to cast itself upon God and His ways as never to expect any comfort or any good but there. Therefore this is what it must rest on forever, and follow after forever.

Third, the soul that follows God fully will follow Him forever, because in fully following the Lord it finds so much ease, peace, joy, and satisfaction that it is forever settled and confirmed in this way. There is never ease, sweetness, and full contentment in God's ways until the heart comes off fully; while it is distracted with jealousies, fears, doubts, lingerings after some other way, many temptations pester the spirit continually. But when it is fully come off, then it goes on with ease; it is satisfied and blesses itself in the way wherein it is. Temptations vanish and the soul is freed from much distraction and trouble.

The ship that is part in the mud and part in the water is quartered up and down, and beats up and down, so that in a little time it beats itself all to pieces. But if it is taken off from the mud and put into the full stream, it goes with ease and safety. Thus it is with a man's heart: while it sticks partly in the mud of the world or the filth of any lust, and conviction of conscience strives to raise it but it is not fully taken off, there is nothing but vexation and trouble in that soul. But when it is taken off and gives itself fully to God in His blessed and holy ways, oh, that sweet and blessed ease that now it finds! When a man halts, the way is tedious to him. He is soon weary and gives over; but when he is sound the way is easy, and he holds on his way to the end. So when there is falseness in men's hearts, they halt in the ways of God. They quickly find them tedious; but others who are of sound spirits find them delightful and go on with strength and hold on to the end. The reason that philosophers give as to why the heavens are incorruptible is that the form of them is so excellent that it wholly fills up the utmost capacity of the matter. So the reason for holding onto an upright heart is the full satisfaction of it, filling up the full capacity of it with contentment and delight in God's ways.

Thus have you heard what it is to follow God fully.

# CHAPTER TWO

# The Excellency of this Frame of Spirit in Four Things

*T*he second point to be propounded in this part is to show wherein the excellency of such a kind of frame of spirit lies. I will describe it in these four things:

1. This is truly to honor God as God: unless God is honored as infinite, He is not honored as God. Now, only by fully following Him do we honor Him as infinite. Where God is not followed thus, He is followed no other than a creature may be followed. This is not therefore to honor Him as God, but rather it is a dishonor to that infinite excellency and blessedness of His whereby He is infinitely above all that creatures are, or that they are in any way capable of. The great thing that God aimed at in creating the heavens and earth was that He might, by angels and men, be honored as God, and therefore that which gives Him this has true and great excellency in it.

2. This full following of God much honors the work of grace and the profession of godliness. It shows a reality, power, excellency, and beauty in it. It shows that it proceeds out of the fullness of Jesus Christ, such as has high and heavenly principles. When there is power, proportion, and constancy in a

man's ways, there must be much beauty in them. There is a forcing of conviction from the consciences of evil men by them. This takes away all pretenses from men, so that they know not how to speak evil of the ways of godliness. They know not how to oppose and persecute them when they can see no flaw, when, though they watch what they can, yet they can see nothing unsuitable to their principles. The principles of godliness for the most part are acknowledged by the consciences of the worst who have any light in them. Therefore, when all a man's ways are suitable to these, it puts wicked men to a stand. They know not what to say against such men, nor against their way; but their own thoughts tell them that surely there is something in these men that has reality, power, and divine excellency in it, that is from none other than God Himself.

3. This has such excellency in it that God Himself boasts of such as these are. As they glory in the Lord and bless themselves in the Lord, so the Lord seems to glory in them and account His name blessed by them. You may see how God rejoices in and makes His boast of Job, Job 1:8: "Hast thou considered my servant Job, that there is none like him in the earth, a perfect and an upright man?" So of David in Acts 13:22: "I have found a man after Mine own heart, which shall fulfill all My will." So of those we read in Revelation 14:4–5: "These are they which were not defiled," and again: "These are they which follow the Lamb whithersoever he goeth." And again in the same verse: "These were redeemed from among men, being the first fruits unto God, and the Lamb, and in their mouth was found no guile."

4. This following of the Lord fully ever attains its end. It prospers in whatever it works for. In whatever thing any soul follows the Lord fully, it shall be sure to accomplish what it aims at and to be satisfied in what it would have. Hosea 6:3:

"Then shall we know, if we follow on to know the Lord." Thus, in Psalm 63, David's soul thirsted after God, his flesh longed for Him, his soul followed after Him. He said himself in the same Psalm that God's right hand now upheld him, and his soul would be satisfied as with marrow and fatness. His mouth would praise the Lord with joyful lips, and the king would rejoice in God.

# CHAPTER THREE

# Rebuke to Divers Sorts Whose Spirits Are Not Full in Following After the Lord

*I*f to follow the Lord fully is so excellent, if this fullness of spirit is such an honor unto God's people, then justly are those rebuked whose spirits are not full in following the Lord, who acknowledge the Lord worthy to be followed but whose spirits are sleight and vain. Their hearts are straitened in the ways of the Lord; they do not fill up this blessed work of following after the Lord; their hearts most basely fall and most miserably vanish in it.

First, some are convinced that their judgments and consciences are for God, but their lusts carry them violently another way. Oh, the miserable torment of these men's spirits while their consciences draw one way and their lusts another! It is not as great an evil to have wild horses tied to the members of one's body, tearing them apart by drawing contrary ways.

Second, others rest in their good inclinations and their good desires. They say they would fain do better, and they hope God will accept the will for the deed. They like God's ways and speak well of good men, and therefore they think their hearts are for God. But these desires and good motions are but as little buds and sprigs that come out of the roots of trees, or from the middle of their body, which come to nothing. They never grow up to bear any fruit. These are far from following the Lord fully and savingly, for:

1. Their judgments are not yet enlightened. They are not thoroughly convinced of the poison and infinite evil there is in sin, or of that absolute, infinite necessity there is in the holy ways of God. They see not the dreadful authority of God in every truth. They think it would be well if things were amended. It would be good if more were done than this: "God help us, we have all our infirmities." And though they do not do as others do, yet they hope their hearts are good towards God. Were it not for some inconveniences they are likely to meet with, they could be content to do more than they do. But what is this to that mighty work of God upon this spirit, convincing of the infinite necessity, equity, and beauty of His blessed ways? What is this to that sight of God's infinite, dreadful authority? Those whose hearts the Lord takes off from other things to work fully after Himself, He begins thus with them in the powerful enlightening and convincing of their judgments.

2. These never were made sensible of their inability to have holy desires after God so as to see any need of any special work of the Holy Ghost to raise such desires in their hearts. Those who are not sensible of their inability to have holy desires, though they may have many flashes like unto holy desires, yet they are wholly strangers to those desires after God which are truly holy.

3. These do not prize the means of grace. They do not long after them. They will not labor; they will not be at charge; they will not endure hardship to attain them; they are not conscionable in the use of them in any power. They do not use all means. If

one way will not bring their desires to effect, they do not try other ways; they are not solicitous about the success of means; they do not look much after them, but rest themselves in the bare use of them, not examining, not searching their hearts to see what is in them that hinders the blessing, not bemoaning their unprofitableness under means.

4. Their desires are not strong or insatiable. Other contentments quiet their hearts. Time wears away the strength of their desires, though they are as far from the enjoyment of the things that were desired as they were at first.

5. Their endeavors are not powerful; they are not working constant endeavors; they do not dedicate, devote, or give themselves up, whatever they are or have, to seeking after the Lord. Their consciences cannot but tell them that the strength of their hearts and endeavors is after other things. David said in Psalm 119:48 that he would lift up his hands unto God's commandments, which he had loved; and he would meditate in His statutes. He did not think it enough to have a love for, to have some wishes and desires to keep God's commandments, but he would lift up his hands to them. He would set himself to work in laboring to obey them. He would meditate, set his mind and thoughts, to plot and contrive, how he might best come to fulfilling them. Psalm 27:4: "One thing have I desired, and that will I seek after." Certainly those slight, vain desires and wishes that are in many people's hearts are not following this blessed God fully. They are but dallyings and triflings with God and their own souls. They are so far from bringing them to God that they prove to be their destruction. "The desire of the slothful killeth him, for his hands refuse to labor" (Proverbs 21:25).

Third, others have good resolutions now and then in some good moods. The truths of God come darting in with some power, as they cannot but yield to them, and then they are resolved that they will do better, that it shall not be with them as it has been. They will set upon a new course of life; things shall be reformed, and their lives shall be changed; but yet these vanish too. They do not follow God fully; they are as those in Deuteronomy 5:27 who seemed to have strong resolutions to walk in God's ways. "Go thus near," they said to Moses, "and hear all that the Lord God shall say, and speak thou unto us all that the Lord our God shall speak unto thee, and we will hear it, and do it." But as the Lord said there concerning them in verse 29, so I may say of these: "Oh, that there were such a heart in them!" How far are they from having yet a heart to follow God fully!

Their resolutions are not fruits of their deep humiliation for their former neglect of God and the former sinfulness of their ways. They are seeking only to procure peace unto themselves for the present, their hearts being stirred by the power of the truth darted in.

They do not arise from changed principles, from a renewed nature, from love for the Lord and His blessed ways. Hence they vanish and they never bring these souls up unto the Lord.

Fourth, others have strong, sudden affections. They feel sometimes some meltings in sorrow for sin, in hearing the blessed truths of God revealed to them. They feel some sweetness in the working of truths upon their hearts. They are sensible of some joys in good things. They have a taste of the powers of the world to come. When they hear Christ preached, or see His body broken or His blood shed in the Sacrament, they think to themselves: "Oh, that Jesus Christ should come from heaven to save such poor wretches as we are, that He should shed His precious blood, that He should die for such vile sinners!" Yet these are a great way off from following the Lord fully.

1. These affections are sudden and flashing. The truths of God pass by them, leaving a little glimmering behind them, or as water passes through a conduit and leaves a dew. But they do not soak into the heart as the water soaks into the earth to make it fruitful.

2. These are stirred with the pardoning, comforting, saving mercies of God, but not with the humbling, renewing, sanctifying mercies. When the Word puts them upon anything that is hard for flesh and blood, it is unsavory to them; their hearts turn from it. If the Word urges strict examination, if it puts them upon finding out the deceits of their spirits, their secret corruptions, and would strain them to higher duties than their principles reach unto, then their spirits fly off. They seek to bless themselves in what they have already, and think that these things trouble people more than needs be. They think: "If God should not be merciful to such who find such affections, such stirrings of heart as we do, then, Lord, what shall become of us?"

3. These fleshly affections arise from spiritual judgment, apprehending the spiritual manner, but their apprehensions of spiritual and heavenly things are too carnal and sensitive. Hence afterwards, when they come to find the good things of the ways of God to be spiritual and heavenly, not suitable to those apprehensions they had of them, their hearts are then taken off as those we read of in John 6:33–34, when Christ told them that "the bread of God is He which cometh down from heaven, and giveth life unto the world."

"Oh," said they, "Lord, ever give us this bread." Their hearts were exceedingly stirred. Christ said in verse 35, "You shall have it, I am the bread of life. He that cometh unto Me shall never hunger. He that believeth in Me shall never thirst." And this is as if He had said, "This must be done by faith. You must feed upon My flesh by faith, and drink My blood by faith."

But now, having apprehended a strange kind of bread from heaven before, and afterwards hearing of nothing other than coming to Christ, and believing in Christ, they were deceived of their expectations, and so were offended. And how their affections fell! For in verse 41 they began to murmur at Him, and in verse 60 they said that it was a hard saying, "who can hear it?" Verse 66: "From that time many of them went back, and walked no more with Him."

The like example we find in Galatians. At first they would have plucked out their eyes for Saint Paul, their affections were so stirred by his ministry. They apprehended some great matters in the message of the gospel that Paul brought; but afterwards, finding that those great and excellent things the gospel spoke of were only spiritual—which their carnal hearts had little skill for, and could not relish—their affections were soon cooled and they fell off from Paul. Take heed, therefore, of resting in these flashy affections, for if you do, when these are gone your hearts will be left in darkness. Many examples are known of such who have proved to be most vile apostates; yet time was wherein they have had many meltings and much sudden strong joy. They have professed that the joy they have found has been so great that if it had continued but a while they could not have lived, but their spirits would have expired.

Think of this as a solid work of the soul proceeding from a humble, broken heart, casting itself upon the faithfulness and freeness of the grace of God in the promise of pardoning and sanctifying mercy, and there resting, willing to venture itself there forever. Though it has no present sense of joy, yet it is far more to be prized than the strongest of these sudden flashes of affection. These flashy affections, that have no principles to maintain them, are like conduits in the city running with wine at the coronation of princes or some other great triumph; but they will not hold. They are like land floods that scream to be a great sea, but come to nothing in a day or two.

There may be flashes of terror and yet no true fear of God. The Israelites were terrified when the Law was given, and yet God said in Deuteronomy 5:29, "Oh, that there were such a heart in them that they would fear Me!" So there may be flashes of joy, desire, sorrow, and yet no true sanctified joy, desire, or sorrow at all. There is much deceit in men's affections. Affections not well principled, not well grounded, soon vanish; time will wear them away. The people of Israel at the giving of the Law had their affections much stirred, so that one would have thought they had been engaged unto the Lord forever. And yet within forty days their hearts were so taken off from God and His Law that it seemed as if God had never made Himself known unto them. They called to Aaron to make them gods to go before them. They said to the molten calf in Exodus 32:4, "These be thy gods, O Israel, which brought thee out of the land of Egypt."

We have another notable example of people whose affections are strong for the present, and yet worn away in a little time, in Hosea 13:1: "When Ephraim spake, trembling, he exalted himself in Israel, but when he offended in Baal, he died." That is, when Jeroboam, who was of the tribe of Ephraim, declared his purpose to alter the worship of God, the people at first were exceedingly affected with it; and they stood all trembling at such a strange thing as that was. The very thought of it made their hearts to shake, because they knew how jealous a God the Lord was. But Jeroboam "exalted himself in Israel." He went on resolutely in his way, and wanted to bring his purpose to effect. Then the people in a little time were brought to offend in Baal, and "then they died." And they became a dead, sottish, heartless people, fit to receive or do anything, though never so vile.

Fifth, others follow the Lord, but they follow Him in a dull, heavy manner. There is no spirit, no heat, no life in their following Him, and therefore they do not follow Him fully. They rest themselves in a middle temper, in a lukewarm course. They well like religion and profession, but what need is there for men to go so far? Why do they need to do so much? As Pharaoh said to the Israelites in Exodus 8:28, "I will let you go, only you shall not go far away." The judgment of these men is for a middle way. They are mixed-spirited men, like Ephraim in Hosea 7:8, mixed among the people. They are as a cake not turned, half-baked and half dough. They go on in an ordinary track of performing the duties of religion without any growth or sensibleness of the want of growth. They set upon some fair way of religion, which they persuade themselves is enough and that they mean to hold to. They are content to make use of Christ and the profession of religion as far as may serve their own turns. But to entertain Christ and His truth as an absolute Lord to rule them, that their spirits cannot bear.

In their conduct there is no ribaldry or filthiness, but neither is there any warmth or heat to refresh and quicken any gracious spirit that has to deal with them. In all the duties of religion that they have to perform, they take no pains to work their hearts to God. Luther calls such kind of men "Cain-ists," that is, they are such as Cain, who offer to God the work done, but do not offer *themselves* to God. They content themselves with general hopes of God's mercy, upon weak and unexamined grounds. They never trouble themselves in calling into question their conditions and eternal estates. They never lay to heart the miseries of God's Church; the public cause of God is not dear unto them. They do not have enough heat to cause a melting spirit for the dishonor that God has by them. Much more is that heat lacking that should keep their hearts melting for the dishonor which God has from others.

Now this temper is so far from following the Lord fully that it is loathsome and abominable to the Lord, so loathsome that He threatens to spew such out of His mouth.

It is observable that, of all the seven churches we read of in Revelation, there is some good said of every one. Each is commended for something except the church of Laodicea, which was a lukewarm church. Of this church there is no good said at all. Yet none of the churches had such a high esteem of itself as this one had. None of them thought themselves to be rich and increased with goods and without need of anything, as this church did. No people so bless themselves in their way as lukewarm people do; and yet no people are more abominable to God than they. What a dishonor the lukewarm temper is to God, as if God were such a God that such flat, slight, dead-hearted formal services as are performed by them were sufficient to honor His holy, great, dreadful, and infinite majesty! God pronounced a curse in Malachi 1:14 against those who did not offer the best they possibly could in sacrifice to Him. And He gave this reason for it: "Because my name is dreadful, and I am a great King, saith the Lord." As if He had said, "Therefore only the most high and excellent things that can be performed by the creature are fit to be rendered up to Me."

This lukewarm temper wrongs Jesus Christ exceedingly, as if there were no other life and virtue in Jesus Christ than to enable a man to do as they do. What? Has Christ laid down His life and shed His precious blood for the renewing of God's image in man, and is it nothing but this? If Christ had never come into the world, men might have done as much as *this* comes to. It is a wrong to the Holy Spirit, likewise, for it is the special office of the Holy Ghost to be a Sanctifier, to frame the heart to God, to quicken the soul with life of grace and holiness, and is this all it does? This would be a poor work if there were nothing more but this.

It dishonors holiness, which is the most glorious thing in the world. The life of God, the divine nature, makes all as if it were nothing more than a moral, lifeless, dead-hearted, empty thing. This puts holiness in subjection to human reason, to carnal wisdom; it must bow to their discretion, to the opinion and ways of men, and, in truth, to their base lusts, even though it is in a more cleanly way than in others. Be convinced, then, that this is not that following the Lord fully which is the honor of God's people in His eyes.

Sixth, some go beyond this dull, lukewarm temper. They are very forward in some things, but in other things their hearts stick. They do not come off fully in them. Agrippa said of himself that Paul had almost persuaded him. The words are: "Thou persuadeth me a little." The hearts of these men are divided, as it is said of those in Hosea 10:2; they will not let go their profession, but will keep their corruption too. Camden reports of Rewald, king of the East Saxons, the first prince of his nation who was baptized, that yet his church had one altar for the Christian religion and another for sacrifices unto devils. Thus these men join religion and their lust together. If they let out their hearts inordinately to any contentment and take liberty sometimes in satisfying some lusts, they think to make up all again by some forwardness and earnest devotion in some other thing. They are like many who get nauseated from overeating and think they can sweat it out and start eating again.

This division of heart the Lord cannot endure, and therefore it follows in that place of Hosea: "They shall be found faulty." Or, as the words are read by some, "Now shall they be made desolate." For in Hebrew the word signifies both to be guilty and to be desolate. It is too much boldness and presumption in men to venture to take liberty to themselves, to choose wherein they will yield to God in some things, but in others to presume to satisfy themselves. This is not to cast down our souls before the Lord as poor, condemned, vile creatures, to lie at His mercy in a humble, faithful resignation of ourselves to Him in all we are or have, which is the honor that God expects from us, and is infinitely due Him.

While our hearts are thus divided between God and other things, God does not account Himself obeyed or honored at all in anything. All that we seem to do in truth is nothing at all. Hence, in Jeremiah 32:23, the prophet charged the people that they neither walked in God's Law, nor had they done anything of all that God had commanded them to do. In verse 30 he said that they had only done evil. In 2 Kings 17, the people are said to fear the Lord and serve their own gods (verse 33); and yet in verse 34 the text says that "they feared not the Lord," showing us that where the heart is divided between God and other things, there God does not have the heart at all. God is not feared; He is not honored at all. If we join the counsels of the flesh with the Spirit, we frustrate all.

Seventh, there are others who cannot be easily convinced in what particulars they forsake God in any of His ways. They seem to have a general forwardness in that which is good, but, the truth is, they follow themselves and not God in all. They rise no higher than self in all they do, which their own consciences, if they are but searched, will tell them. The commandment of God may be made the pretense, but self is the chief engine; self is the great mover in all. Physicians put many operative ingredients into their medicine, and they are the things that work; but besides those, they put in something to give a little color or taste, which does neither any good nor harm. They have no operation at all.

Thus it is in many men's religion: self-ends are the operative ingredients in what they do, and the show of obedience to God is but that which gives the color. That which they do may have the better appearance. It is impossible that a man who seeks himself should come up to this fullness of spirit that is required in this following of the Lord. In Hosea 10:1 it is said that Israel is an empty vine. Why so? "He bringeth forth fruit unto himself." He brings forth fruit but yet is empty, because he brings it forth unto himself. Where self-ends are the chief movers, there is no further latitude or degree of godliness minded but such as may be serviceable unto them. Now they cannot but be low, strait, and narrow in comparison to those who lift up God in all they do. Therefore their profession must be empty and scant, not full and powerful as it is in the other.

A self-seeking heart is always an empty heart, but a gracious heart is fruitful in all manner of pleasant fruits, new and old. And what is the reason? "I have laid them up for thee, O my beloved" (Song of Solomon 7:13). Observe the difference: Israel is an empty vine; he brings forth fruit to himself. But the church here brings forth all manner of pleasant fruit, for she lays them up for her beloved. She brings them not forth for herself, as Israel did.

Eighth, others follow the Lord earnestly for a while, but afterwards they forsake Him. They turn apostate; they do not fill up the work they have begun, but undo all again. Of these it may be said as it was of those in Lamentations 4:7–8. They were whiter than milk; they were as rubies and polished sapphires with regard to their glorious profession; but now they are blacker than coal. God may justly complain of them, as He did of His people in Micah 2:8: "They who were My people yesterday are now risen up against Me as an enemy." It was far otherwise with them very lately than it is now. Many are very hopeful at first, yet they prove exceedingly vile afterwards. Yea, the more forward in good at first, the more vile afterwards. Water that has once been heated and grows cold again is colder than ever it was before.

It is reported that Nero, who proved the very monster of men for wickedness, yet in the first five years of his reign behaved himself exceedingly well; in fact, so much so that it was used as a proverb to express the good beginnings of men: "Nero's five first years." So it was with Caligula, who proved afterwards exceedingly wicked, yet Josephus reports that when he was young he traveled very diligently in good disciplines; he was of sweet conversation, modest, and he governed the empire the first two years of his reign with most noble directions, behaving himself graciously towards all men.

Yea, Julian himself, who proved to be such a cursed apostate, yet when he was young was very forward and hopeful. He was a public reader of Holy Scripture in the church. He seemed to glory in nothing more than in religion. He was of a very temperate diet, content with mean food, without much preparation. He used to lie hard in mean bedding, to watch much at night, and to spend his time in study. He was very chaste, clear from the least suspicion of lust. Those officers who were with him, who served for nothing but to maintain delicacy and luxury, he banished from him. He took no delight in public shows. When he came to them, he came rather out of necessity than for any pleasure he took in them. He said that when he was in the theater, he was more like a detester of plays than a spectator of them. He said that he was present at them with trouble and disdain, and was joyful when he went from them. He loved learning exceedingly much. Hearing of a philosopher who came to him out of Asia, he leapt out of the door, went to meet him, kissed him, and entertained him with much honor.

In an epistle of his to one Ecdicius, a governor of Egypt, he had this notable expression: "Some delight in horses, others in birds, others in beasts; but I from my very childhood have burned with desire after books."

He had an honorable esteem of man's soul, looking upon the body as vile in comparison to it. There is this notable expression reported of him concerning this: "It is a shameful thing for any wise man, seeing he hath a soul, to seek for praises from anything that belongs to his body." He seemed to have much uprightness in the course of justice. He would not condemn upon accusations without proof. On one occasion, one Delphidius accused a man brought before Julian of a crime of which he could not bring sufficient proof. The party accused denied the fact, and this Delphidius answered, "If it be sufficient to deny that which is laid to one's charge, who shall be found guilty?" Then Julian answered, "And if it be sufficient to be accused, who can be innocent?"

Many other notable things are reported of him, but these I have related more fully because in this example we may see how far a man may go in much seeming good, what hopeful beginnings he may have, and yet what a vile, cursed monster he may prove to be if he looks not to it. Let none then rest themselves in their good beginnings; but as they have made entrance upon this work in following the Lord, so let them labor to fill it up. And as for those who heretofore have seemed to be forward and hopeful while they lived in families, and under the care and watchful eye of able and godly men, and yet have now forsaken the Lord and His ways, let such know that it is an evil and bitter thing to forsake the blessed God, to turn from Him to follow after vanities that cannot profit. So great an evil is it that God Himself calls the heavens to be astonished at this. Jeremiah 2:12–13: "Be astonished, O ye heavens, at this, and be horribly afraid, be ye very desolate, saith the Lord: for my people have committed two evils; they have forsaken Me the fountain of living waters, and hewed them out cisterns, broken cisterns, that can hold no water." The evil of this forsaking the Lord would be great, even if this were all.

First, know that all your labor in religion, all that you have done is lost. Hosea 8:2: "Israel shall cry to me, My God, we know thee"; but verse 3: "Israel hath cast off the thing that is good." Therefore verse 7 says that "they have sown the wind, and shall reap the whirlwind." It is but sowing to the wind to follow God in some things and not to hold on in our way. 2 John 8: "Look to yourselves that we lose not those things that we have wrought." It is an evil thing to lose all that we have wrought for, but this is not all.

Second, if you leave off following the Lord, all the good that you have ever done and made profession of shall serve only to aggravate your sin and increase your torment.

Third, this leaving off from following the Lord is a great dishonor to God and His ways. It is an upbraiding of them, as if they were not good enough to draw the heart constantly after them; as if there were not that in them that they make show for. Hence the Lord pleads with His people who had forsaken Him in Jeremiah 2:5: "What iniquity have your fathers found in Me, that they are gone far from Me, and have walked after vanity?" It is as if He had said, "The world may think My ways are not equitable; men may think that I have not shown Myself a God ready to do good and reward those who follow Me." Hebrews 6:6 says that the forsaking of the truth, the profession whereof we have once taken up, puts Christ to open shame.

Fourth, such men as these do much mischief in the world.

They are grievous scandals. They make the good ways of God to be evil spoken of. They harden men's hearts against them, and against the profession of them. Many in hell curse them as the cause of their ruin. If a man were born to do mischief, he could not do greater in any way than this. So much hurt is done by them. They cause such blemishes, such spots to be upon the profession of godliness, that we should be glad if we could wash them off with our dearest heart-blood and account it well bestowed. But woe to them by whom these offenses come. The greatest part of all the scorn, contempt of, and opposition against the ways of God and godly men shall be charged upon these men as the causes of it. For were it not for such as these, wicked men could not tell what to say for themselves in their opposition to those ways of godliness, which in themselves are so good and blessed. Woe to them by whom such offenses come.

Fifth, these men shall have their spirits filled with horror. They did not fill up their work in following the Lord, but God and conscience shall follow them with anguish and horror and fill up their spirits with them. It may be that once they had some flashing comforts in the performance of some duties; but they shall be all taken from them; and dismal horror and hideous amazement of spirit shall possess them. Proverbs 14:14: "The backslider in heart shall be filled with his own ways." Much more, then, the backslider in heart and life too shall be filled; he shall have enough of them.

Conscience one day will upbraid, fly in the face, and tear the heart: "O wretched creature, what have you done? Whom have you forsaken? Is it not the God of life, peace, comfort, and all good that you have forsaken? Are they not the blessed ways of holiness, the ways of eternal rest and peace that you have left? God has likewise forsaken you, and all good and comfort have begun to withdraw themselves from you. You are likely to be left in horrid, dismal darkness. It is just that you should be left as a forsaken, forlorn, miserable wretch who has thus wretchedly and vilely forsaken God and His truth for the enjoyment of such poor, base things as your heart is turned aside to. How will you be able to look upon the faces of those with whom you formerly joined in holy duties, and had communion with? But how can you look upon the face of the blessed God when He shall appear in His glory unto you? What anguish will it be to you when you shall see others, who have continued in their way following the Lord, to be forever blessed in that God whom their souls have followed and cleaved constantly unto? But you, because your base, unbelieving heart dared not venture all upon Him, now you are cast out forever with an eternal curse."

Oh, what a rack of conscience will it be when you shall see in what a fair way you once were; but for want of coming off fully and constantly in such and such particulars, you are now forever lost!

Last, these men are hateful both to God and men. They are hateful to men because they go so far, and to God because they go no further. Hebrews 10:38: "If any man draw back, My soul shall have no pleasure in him."

Oh, what a happy thing it would be if God would trouble the ways of these poor creatures; if He would make them bitter and grievous to them; if He would magnify His mercy and power in turning their hearts again towards Him; if He would deal with them as He did with His people in Hosea 2:6–7: "Hedge up their ways with thorns, make a wall that they should not find their paths," that they might at length come to that blessed resolution we find there: "I will go and return to my husband, for then it was better with me than now.

Then they might say, "So I will go and return to my former ways, and follow after the Lord again, from whom I have wretchedly departed, for then it was better with me than it is now. Then I had more comfort, more peace, more safety, more blessing than I have now."

And let such know that it would be just with God forever to reject those who have forsaken Him, just to say that vanity should be their portion who have turned after lying vanities. And many of the ancients have made the case of such exceedingly doubtful, especially if after conviction they have forsaken God again and again. Clemens Alexandrinus thought that God might give such the first and second repentance, but if they fell more often there was no renewing them by repentance. Origen seemed likewise to be of the same mind, in his fifth homily upon Leviticus, chapter 25. So said Tertullian in his book on repentance: "God grant a second repentance, but no further." Thus we see the strictness of these ancient times.

But though these words may leave these men exceedingly comfortless, yet let them know that the Lord calls them to return again unto Himself. Jeremiah 3:1: "For though it be that if a wife hath played the harlot, and she be put away and become another man's, her husband will not receive her again"; yet, said the Lord in the same place, "Thou hast played the harlot with many lovers, but yet return to me." And verse 22: "Return, ye backsliding children, and I will heal your backslidings."

Oh, that your hearts would answer as theirs there did! Oh, that this gracious offer of the Lord might have the same effect upon your hearts as it had upon theirs! "Behold," said they, "we come unto Thee, for Thou art the Lord our God. Truly in vain is salvation hoped for from the hills. We see that we have been utterly deceived. The ways that we have chosen have not been good. Shame has devoured our labor; we have bestowed our labor on shameful things; we lie down in our shame, and our confusion covers us, for we have sinned against the Lord our God."

When a man goes from the sun, the sunbeams follow him, shine on him, and warm him. So though you have departed from the Lord, yet the beams of God's mercy this day follow you; they shine on you. Oh, that they might so warm your heart as to cause you to return.

# CHAPTER FOUR

# Comfort and Encouragement to Those Who Follow the Lord Fully

*I*f this following the Lord fully is the honor of the saints before the Lord, then here is comfort and encouragement to those whose conscience witnesses that their hearts and ways are fully after the Lord. Whatever others do, yet there is a generation of men in the world who fully follow the Lord. Blessed are you of the Lord; you are honorable in the eyes of God and man; you make up in part the hurt that is done to religion by others; you bind up the wounds of Jesus Christ and in part heal His scars. If you are content to give up all to God, to trust God with all, know that there are many blessed promises full of mercy and encouragement for you, that God will make good to the full unto you. Yea, they shall come to you more full of goodness and blessing than you can imagine.

Caleb challenged this promise of God made to him in this place upon this ground (Joshua 14:8), forty-five years after it was made. For he was but forty years old when he went to spy out the land, and when he challenged this promise in this place he said, verse 10, "I am this day four score and five years old." Though

God may seem to defer a while the fulfilling of His promise, yet be encouraged to follow Him still, for the eye of God is upon you to make good His word unto you; and the longer it stays, the more full with good and blessing it will come. God seemed to defer a long time the promise He made to Abraham, that He would make His seed as the stars of heaven. For two hundred and fifteen years after this promise was made there were but seventy souls that came out of Abraham's loins, namely, when Jacob went down into Egypt. If we compute the time, we shall find it to be just two hundred and fifteen years; for Abraham was seventy-five years old when the promise was made. He was a hundred years old when Isaac was born. Isaac was forty years old before he married, and he continued twenty years without a child. Jacob was one hundred and thirty years old when he went into Egypt. So the time turns out to be exactly two hundred and fifteen years, which was just half the time from the promise till the people of Israel came out of Egypt, which Paul said in Galatians 3:17 was four hundred and thirty years.

Now observe that, whereas God half this time did but little for Abraham in the fulfilling of this promise, yet because Abraham followed Him fully and ventured himself wholly upon the faithfulness of the Lord, God came in fully with His mercy at the last. For, in the second two hundred and fifteen years, he so increased his seed that from seventy souls they were grown up to be six hundred three thousand, five hundred fifty (Numbers 1:45–46). And this number includes only those from twenty years old and upward, such men as were able to go to war; there were this many of these, besides all children and women which, it is likely, were by far the greater number. Yea, and the tribe of Levi was not numbered among this number; there were upwards of twenty-two thousand besides. Thus you see how fully God comes in at the last in His mercy, making good His word of promise to such who follow Him fully.

Be as full as you can in following the Lord, and the Lord will be as full towards you in doing good to you. God's mercy shall be ever as full as your obedience can be. 2 Samuel 22:26: "with the upright Thou wilt show Thyself upright." The words in the original are: "with the strong and perfect, Thou wilt show thyself strong and perfect." God will go on strongly to His perfection of mercy towards those who go on strongly in their perfection of obedience towards Him. Psalm 11:7: "The Lord loveth righteousness, and His countenance doth behold the upright." The word-for-word translation is: "The Lord loveth righteousness, and His face shall behold the upright."

"Righteousness" is when all the duties of righteousness are together.

"And his face shall behold" represents all the several kinds and manners of the blessed, comfortable manifestations of His love the upright shall have. The great difficulties you meet with in God's ways (if you are not discouraged, but go through them) shall turn to your greatest comforts. Caleb was not discouraged by the Anakims, those great giants, and the strong places they lived in, which so discouraged the rest. Therefore Hebron, the place of the giants, was given to him for a possession (Joshua 14:12–15).

God certainly will remember the kindness of those who are willing to follow Him through the wilderness of difficulties and discouragements (Jeremiah 2:2). You who do this shall die without stain, without any blur, which few do. Your memories shall be sweet and blessed when you are dead and gone. You shall have "an entrance ministered unto you abundantly, into the everlasting kingdom of our Lord and Savior Jesus Christ" (2 Peter 1:11). This is promised not only to those who are godly, but who abound in godliness, as in verse 8. They shall be as a ship coming gloriously into the haven with full sail. Thus Paul, in 2 Timothy 4:7–8, with much confidence and full assurance concludes that since he had fought the good fight, finished his course, and kept the faith, henceforth there was laid up for him a crown of righteousness, which the righteous Judge should give him at that day. He challenged it upon the righteousness of God.

When the souls of those who have followed God fully are to enter into heaven, the everlasting doors shall stand wide open for them. When great men come to a house, the great gates are set open for their entrance. And in heaven, oh, how full a reward shall there be there for them (2 John 8)! "There is fullness of joy at God's right hand" (Psalm 16:11). It shall be so full as shall be more than can enter into them. They must enter into it because it cannot enter into them. There they shall not taste of joy and happiness, but shall be filled up with them. This Christ encouraged His disciples with in Luke 22:28–29: "Ye are they which have continued with Me in My temptations, and I appoint unto you a kingdom as My Father hath appointed unto Me." With this, Paul encouraged himself in the afflictions he met with while he was following the Lord. 2 Corinthians 4:17: "For our light affliction, which is but for a moment, worketh for us a far more exceeding eternal weight of glory."

First, it is glory; and this word alone implies that there is exceedingly much in it. But further, it is a weight of glory, yea, an eternal weight of glory; and more than that, it is an exceeding weight of glory. And as if it yet were not expressed fully enough, he adds further that it is a far more exceeding eternal weight of glory. And what expression can be fuller than this? This was what likewise encouraged Moses in his following the Lord, forsaking the pleasures, the riches and treasures of Egypt that he might follow the Lord fully. "For he had a respect unto the recompense of the reward" (Hebrews 11:26). And you whose hearts and ways are fully after the Lord have more cause to rejoice in your blessedness because it is the blessedness but of a few. "Iniquity shall abound," said Christ in Matthew 24: 12–13, "and the love of many shall wax cold, but he that endures to the end shall be saved." It is "but he," in the singular number, who endures to the end.

Let these encouragements then fill your hearts with joy, and your spirits with renewed resolutions and vigor to fill up your course. Let them fill your sails that you may go on with strength and prosper and be forever blessed in your way.

I conclude this use with what the apostle said in 2 Corinthians 7:1: "Seeing we have these promises (these encouragements) let us labor to perfect our holiness in the fear of God." And thus I pass to the last use, which is of exhortation.

# CHAPTER FIVE

# An Exhortation to Follow the Lord Fully

Now may the Lord carry our hearts fully after Himself. The two blind men in Matthew 20 followed Christ as soon as their eyes were opened. So, were our eyes opened, we would certainly follow after the Lord. Were they fully opened our hearts would follow fully. Many of you have some convictions, some inclinations, stirrings of affections, and good resolutions; you begin to have good thoughts of God's ways; you are always persuaded. Oh, that the work were thoroughly done! It is a pity but that these beginnings should be improved. When Christ saw the good inclinations of the young man who came to Him, the text says, "He looked upon him, and loved him." Those beginnings are lovely; but how lovely then would the full work be if these beginnings were brought to perfection?

In this use we shall show:

1. The motives that may draw our hearts to follow the Lord fully.

2.   What it is that hinders the soul in this work, and how it may be prevented.

3.   What it is that would bring off the heart fully indeed.

1. As for the motives that may draw our hearts to follow the Lord fully, there is infinite reason that our hearts should be fully after the Lord, for:

First, there is a fullness of all good in God. He is worthy. "Thou art worthy, O Lord, to receive glory, honor, and power (Revelation 4:11)." He is worthy to receive the highest honor that any of His creatures can by any means give unto Him. The heathen gods were honored as those who were only authors of some particular good things, and therefore there were such a multiplicity of them. One was honored as the author of one good thing and another as the author of another; and therefore particular honor was sufficient for them. There was no reason that any of them should have the whole soul, working the fullness of the operations of it after them; but our God is not so. He is a universal good in whom there is all good, from whom all good flows, and by whom all good is preserved in the being it has. And therefore it is most absolute, universal honor and service that are due to Him.

If we had a thousand souls, and if they were all of ten thousand times larger extent than they are, yet there would be infinite reason that they should all, in their full latitude, extent, and strength, follow after our God, to honor, magnify, and worship this God forever. As one blessed martyr once said, "What have I but one life to lay down for Christ? If I had as many lives as there are hairs upon my head, they should all go for Jesus Christ." He saw Christ worthy of all he had, yea, of more than he had. This was God's own argument to Abraham in Genesis 17:1, "Walk before me, and be upright." Be perfect, for I am God all-sufficient. I have all perfection *in* Me, and therefore be perfect *before* Me.

Second, consider that God might have had full glory in your destruction. Let Him not be a loser in showing mercy to you.

How much better is it for you that He should have the fullness of His glory in His mercy to you than the fullness of it in His judgments upon you? This He might have had long ago, yea, and the fullness of His glory He will have. If you do not give it to Him, He will force it from you.

Third, Christ has fully gone through the great work of redemption. He would never leave it till He had fully accomplished all and said, "It is finished." This was a mighty work, for the accomplishment whereof He passed through more difficulties than you are ever likely to do in the fullest measure of following the Lord that possibly can be.

Fourth, God's mercies for the present are very full towards you: His pardoning mercies and His supplying mercies, with all things needful. When He receives you to mercy, He fully pardons all your sins. He leaves nothing upon the score. He remits all your punishments.

This was David's argument in Psalm 103:1–3: "Bless the Lord, O my soul, and all that is within me, bless his Holy Name." And "bless the Lord, O my soul" again. As if he should say, "Oh, let God be fully blessed by me." Why? What was it that raised and enlarged David's heart? It follows: "Who forgiveth all thine iniquities, and healeth all thy diseases." And verse 4: "He crowneth thee with lovingkindnesses." And verse 5: "He satisfieth thy mouth with good things." God gives His servants fullness in all they enjoy. His grace exceedingly abounds towards them in everything.

2 Corinthians 9:8 is very remarkable for setting out the abounding of God's grace towards His people: "And God is able to make all grace abound towards you, that ye, always having all sufficiency in all things, may abound to every good work." Whatever God is able to do for us, by faith we make it as if it were done. And this power of God is set forth to the

Corinthians as a motive to persuade them to full obedience, that they might abound in every good work; which, if they did, they would have this power of God active and fully working for them according to these large expressions we have of it in this Scripture. And observe the several expressions:

It is grace.
Then all grace.
Then all grace abounding.
A sufficiency.
An all-sufficiency.
An all-sufficiency in all things.
Always an all-sufficiency in all things.

And is not here an argument full enough to cause them and us, and all God's people forever, to abound in every good work? How often does God fill our cup with mercy and even make it run over, as in Psalm 23:5? If there shall be an all-sufficiency in all things, then there will be an all-sufficiency in our greatest straits, in our greatest afflictions, in our greatest fears. It is said of the wicked in Job 20:22, "In the fullness of his sufficiency, he shall be in straits." The contrary is true concerning God's people. In the fullness of their straits, they shall be in all-sufficiency. God causes all His attributes, all the ways of His providence, and all His creatures to work for the good of His people. All that is in God, all that God does, and all that belongs to God are for them. Therefore there is infinite reason that all they are, all they do, and all they have should work for His honor.

All that there is in God is for them. Jeremiah 32:41: "I will rejoice over them to do them good, and I will plant them in this land assuredly, with My whole heart, and with My whole soul." God calls for no more from you than He is willing to give unto you. He would have your whole heart and your whole soul for His honor, and He promises to give you His whole heart and His whole soul for your good. Again, all that God does is for you. Psalm 25:10: "All the paths of the Lord are mercy and truth, unto such as keep His covenant and His testimonies." The paths of the Lord are the ways of God in the passages of His providence; not only some particular acts, but the track of God in His ways, His paths. Now all these paths of God, that is, all the workings of God in the ways of His providence, are mercy unto such as obey Him. They work mercifully for their good. And further observe that they are not only mercy, but mercy in truth, that they should thus work for them. God has tied this mercy to us by His truth.

See here the difference between God's mercy to His people and His mercy to other men. Some of God's paths may be mercy to other men, but not all, or some particular acts of God rather than His paths. God does not ordinarily go on in a track and course of His mercies with them as He does with His people. As their obedience is only in some particular acts and no continued course, so God's mercy to them, which comes from His general bounty, is manifested only in some particular acts of His and not in any constant course. But it is otherwise in His dealings towards His people. They go on in a constant course of obedience. They make God's commandments their paths, and therefore God goes on in a constant course of lovingkindness towards them. He makes His mercy to them the ordinary paths wherein He walks with them. Psalm 36:10: "Oh, continue Thy lovingkindness to them that know Thee, and Thy righteousness to the upright in heart." The word in the original is: "Draw out Thy lovingkindness." God's mercies to His own are a continued series; they are drawn out from a constant spring; they come forth from a never-failing fountain. There is a connection for His people between one mercy and another; but as for others, God now and then only casts His favors on them.

Second, all God's paths are mercy to His people, not some few. There are none of God's dealings but aim at good towards them. If God should cause one favor to follow another towards some wicked man out of the fullness of His bounty, yet it cannot be said of any wicked man in the world that all the paths of God are mercy towards him. God has His paths of wrath and judgment wherein He is coming towards him, though he is little aware of it. But this blessing of the paths of God being mercy is a peculiar blessing to such as follow the Lord fully in the uprightness of their hearts, in all the paths of service and obedience.

And, third, observe yet a greater difference than the former: all the paths of God are not only mercy, but mercy and truth to His people. Though God may show mercy to others, yet He has not tied His mercy to them by His truth. They cannot challenge mercy from Him by virtue of His truth. If they have mercy, it is more than they could have expected. They cannot be sure of it one hour. They have nothing to show for their mercy. They do not hold their mercy upon that tenor of God's truth that His people do. Nay, when God comes to make good His truth, to give His truth the glory it deserves, then there is an end put to their mercy; it is cut off from them. But there is a blessed connection between mercy and truth in the good that God's people enjoy. According to the like expression in the forenamed Psalm 36:10, the lovingkindness and the righteousness of God are put together as the portion of an upright heart. And hence the mercies they have are no other than such as they may expect, as they may build upon before they come, such as are made over to them by the truth of God. And when they are come, they may be sure to hold them because they hold them upon such a blessed tenure of God's own truth. And hence the Scripture calls them "sure mercies." See how confident David was of holding God's mercies. Psalm 23:6: "Surely goodness and mercy shall follow me all the days of my life."

Further, all that God has is for their good. The heavens and earth and all creatures are theirs and work continually for them. Hosea 2:21–22: "I will hear the heavens, and they shall hear the earth, and the earth shall bear the corn, and the wine, and the oil, and they shall hear Jezreel." 1 Corinthians 3:22–23: "The world, life, death, things present, things to come, all are yours and ye are Christ's, and Christ is God's." Romans 8:28: "And we know that all things work together for good to them that love God." This is a mystery that the world is not acquainted with, but we know it, said the apostle. The world may think that things work against us. Yea, all things in the world seem to work against us; but we know that all things do work for good, and they work together for good.

Though some particular things considered apart may work for good to other men, yet all together works for good to us. Although the good does not seem yet to come forth, yet it is working for us. Stay till the work is done and it will appear. It will be good. Though it may be not the same good that we think of, yet it will be a good that will be better for us, a greater good than we imagined or desired.

Now, then, if all that is God's is for you, and works thus fully for you, is there not reason then that all that is yours should be for God and work as fully for Him? Yours, did I say? The truth is, there is nothing that is yours. For all is God's. God has a greater propriety in, and right to, whatever you are and have than you do; but God is pleased to let it be called yours that you may freely give it to Him. And if it is His own, why should He not have it fully? If He thus enlarges Himself towards you, how inequitable is it that you should be scant in your service to Him, and in things honoring to Him?

Wicked men fully follow after that which is evil. It would be an infinite shame and confusion then to us, an infinite dishonor likewise unto God, if we should not as fully follow the Lord in that which is good! Ecclesiastes 9:3: "The heart of the sons of men is full of evil." And 8:11: "The heart of the sons of men is fully set in them to do evil." The Septuagint translates this: "The heart of man hath a plerophory to evil." It is set upon it without any doubt or suspicion. There is a plerophory, a full persuasion of boldness, to sin in them. Why should there not be a plerophory, a full persuasion, of faith in God's servants to that which is good? Micah 7:3 says that wicked men do evil with both hands earnestly. In Isaiah 57:5 idolaters are said to inflame themselves with their idols. In Jeremiah 8:2 they are said, (1) to love their idols; (2) to serve them; (3) to walk after them; (4) to seek them; and (5) to worship them. All these five expressions together in one verse set forth the earnestness and fullness of the spirit of idolaters towards their idols. Where have we five such expressions together to set out the fullness of the work of men's spirits in following after the Lord?

It was said that Ahab sold himself to work wickedness. What a fullness of spirit was there in him in doing wickedness! Jeremiah 23:10 says there of the people that their course was evil and their force was not right. That is, the strength and force that was in their spirits was not right; it was not after God, but after the ways of sin. How many difficulties will men pass through for their lusts! What cost will they incur! How great things will they suffer! Nothing is so dear unto them but they will be content to part with it for, and bestow it upon, their idols. How soon did the people in Exodus 32 break off their golden earrings from their ears to make an idol with, and shall not then our hearts and lives be more fully after the blessed God? We see wicked men stick close to their wicked principles. They are bold; they will not be daunted; they will go through with the work they have begun, whatever comes of it. Should not we much more stick to our principles? Should not we much more be undaunted in our way and go through with our work?

I remember reading a passage in St. Cyprian where he brings in the devil triumphing over Christ in this manner: "As for my followers, I never died for them as Christ did for His. I never promised them so great reward as Christ has done to His; and yet I have more followers than He, and they do more for me, than His do for Him." Oh, let the thought of our giving the devil occasion thus to triumph over Christ in our slackness and negligence in following after Him cause shame and confusion to cover our faces.

And yet, to pursue this argument a little more closely: it may be you heretofore have lived sinfully; your hearts have been strong after evil and your lives have been fruitful in it. It may be you have been forward in putting forth yourselves as ringleaders in that which was evil, not only stout and perverse yourselves, but maintainers and encouragers of much evil in others. You gave up your members, your estates, and what you had to the service of sin. Much time was spent, much sleep lost, in plotting and contriving wickedness, much pains taken in the execution of it; and now your hearts and ways seem to be for God. And is a poor, slight, scant, dead-hearted service sufficient for Him? Oh, be ashamed and confounded in your thoughts! Let conscience judge between God and His creature. Do you thus requite the Lord? Is this your kindness to Him? Is there not infinite reason that, as you have yielded your members as servants to uncleanness, and to iniquity unto iniquity, even so you now should yield your member as servants to righteousness unto holiness?

Look at Romans 6:19 and mark the opposition there. There are three *to's* in the expressions of the service to sin, *to* uncleanness, *to* iniquity, *unto* iniquity; but in the service of God there are only two, *to* righteousness and *unto* holiness. It is true, in this life there will never be that fullness of spirit in following after God as there was in following after sin because there was nothing but sin in the soul before; no other stream to abate it. But now there is something else besides grace: a stream of corruption to oppose it. Yet we should be ashamed that there should be such a difference. The thought of it should cause a dejection of heart within us, and we should judge it infinitely equitable and reasonable that we should endeavor to the utmost we are able to follow God as fully now as ever we followed sin before. Paul, in Acts 26:11, confessed that in his former way he was mad in the persecution of God's servants; and, when God turned the stream, others judged him as mad in the other way. 2 Corinthians 5:13–14: "For whether we be besides ourselves, it is to God; the love of Christ constraineth us." And hence we may observe that the same word that signifies to persecute, he uses to set out his earnest pressing towards the mark. Philippians 3:14: "I press towards the mark, for the prize of the high calling of God." The word that is there translated "press towards" is the same that signifies to persecute, because the earnestness of his spirit, in pressing towards the mark now, is the same that it was in his persecution of those who pressed towards the mark before.

The more fully we follow God, the more full shall our present peace, joy, and soul-satisfying contentment be. Psalm 119:130: "The entrance of Thy words giveth light." The beginning of following God is sweet and good, but the further we go on the more sweetness we shall find, as they who walked toward Zion. Psalm 84:7: "They went from strength to strength." Those who walk after the Lord go from peace to peace, from joy to joy, from one degree of comfort unto another; for if the entrance into our way is so good and sweet, what will it be when we come into the midst of it? Proverbs 8:20: "I lead in the way of righteousness, in the midst of the judgment." Mark what follows in verse 21: "That I might cause those that love me to inherit substance, and I will fill their treasures." Then doth the soul inherit substance indeed; then are the treasures of it filled: when wisdom leads it not only in the way of righteousness, but in the midst of the paths of judgment.

The way of the just is compared to the shining of the light "that shineth more and more unto the perfect day" (Proverbs 4:18). The further he goes on his way, the more light he has and the more gloriously it shines upon him. Psalm 36:8: "They shall be abundantly satisfied and they shall drink of the river of pleasures." Who are those that shall be thus abundantly satisfied, and shall have this river of pleasures? They are, verse 10, "the upright in heart." The soul that walks on before the Lord in uprightness shall not want satisfaction, shall not want pleasure. Psalm 119:165: "Great peace have they which love Thy law." It is more to love God's law than to do the thing that is commanded in it. The soul that not only submits to the Law but loves it will be abundant in duty, for love is bountiful; and great peace has such a soul, that thus loves God's Law.

Every good motion in the soul is as the bud of the Lord, and that is beautiful and glorious; but how excellent and glorious is the fruit of it then! The good beginnings, which are as the budding of the pomegranate and the putting forth of the tender vine, are delightful to God and the soul. But how pleasant then is the fruit when it comes to ripeness!

The more fully we follow on in God's ways, the more full will the testimony of the witnesses both in heaven and earth be in witnessing our blessed estate unto us. Those three witnesses in heaven—the Father, Word, and Holy Ghost—and those three on earth—the Spirit, water, and the blood—of which John spoke in 1 John 5:7–8 will all come with their full testimony to that soul which follows God fully. By following the Lord fully, we keep our evidences clear. Sin blots and blurs our evidences, so that oftentimes we cannot read them; but when the heart keeps close to God, and walks fully with Him, then all is kept fair. The Kingdom of God consists in righteousness, peace, and joy. The more fully we are brought into His Kingdom, the more fully we are under His government. As there will be the more righteousness, so the more peace and joy. Isaiah 9:7: "Of the increase of his government, and peace, there shall be no end." The more increase there is of Christ's government in the soul, the more full it is and the more peace will be there.

There is great reason that we should walk fully after the Lord, because the way that God calls us to walk in is a most blessed and holy way. In Revelation 21:21, the streets of Jerusalem (that is, the ways of God's people in His Church, wherein they are to walk) are said to be of pure gold, and, as it were, transparent glass. They are golden ways; they are bright, shining ways. Proverbs 3:17: "The ways of wisdom are the ways of pleasantness, and all her paths are peace." There is no one command of God, where He would have us follow Him, but it is very lovely; there is much good in it. God requires nothing of us but that which is most just and holy. As God is holy in all His works, so He is holy in all His commands. They are no other but that which, if our hearts were as they ought, we would choose for ourselves. A righteous man is a law to himself; he sees that good, that beauty, that equity in all God's laws as he would choose for Himself were he left at his own liberty. What one thing is there in God's law that could be spared? What is there that you could be glad to be exempt from? It may be in the strength of temptation, when some lust is up working, the flesh would fain have some liberty; but upon due serious thoughts, looking into the bottom of things, a gracious soul closes with the Law and loves it as gold, yea, fine gold. That soul breaks for the longing it has, not to reward for obedience to God's statutes and judgments, but to the statutes and judgments of God themselves, as David said his soul did.

However rugged and hard our path in following the Lord may seem to the flesh, with regard to the afflictions and troubles it meets with in the way, yet where there is a spiritual eye, the way of holiness appears exceedingly lovely and beautiful. Though David in Psalm 23 supposed the worst that might befall him in his way, as that he might walk through the valley of the shadow of death, yet he called his way "green pastures" and said that God would lead him by the still waters. It is true, the ways of God are grievous to the wicked, but very good and delightful to the saints because they are the ways of holiness. Isaiah 35:8: "And a highway shall be there, and it shall be called the way of holiness. The unclean shall not pass over it."

The consideration of the end of our way should be a strong motive to draw our hearts fully after the Lord in it. The entrance into it is sweet, the midst of it more, as before we have shown, but the end of it most sweet of all. There is that coming which will fully recompense all.

Consider the sweetness of the end of our way, first, in that period of it that will be at death, and, second, in that glorious reward we shall have in heaven.

The sweet and blessed comfort that fully following the Lord brings at death is enough to recompense all the trouble and hardship that we meet with in our way while we are following Him. This has caused many saints of God to lie triumphing when they have been upon their deathbeds, blessing the Lord that ever they knew His ways, that ever He drew their hearts to follow after Him in them.

When Hezekiah received the message of death (Isaiah 38:2–3), he turned his face to the wall and said, "Remember, O Lord, I beseech Thee, how I have walked before Thee in truth, and with a perfect heart, and have done that which is good in Thy sight." And Hezekiah wept sorely. Oh, the sweetness that possessed the heart of Hezekiah, which flowed from the testimony of his conscience that he had fully walked after the Lord with a perfect heart! The verb there, "I have walked," is in that mood in the original that adds to the significance of it. It signifies: "I have continually without ceasing walked."

Luther was a man whose spirit was exceedingly full in his love unto, and walking after, the Lord Jesus Christ while he lived. And when he came to die, his spirit was full of comfort and joy and courage. These expressions broke forth from him: "O my heavenly Father, O God the Father of the Lord Jesus Christ, the God of all comfort, I give Thee thanks that Thou hast revealed Thy Son Jesus Christ to me, whom I have believed, whom I have professed, whom I have loved, whom I have honored, whom the Bishop of Rome, and the rest of the crowd of the wicked men have persecuted and condemned; and now I beseech Thee, O my Lord Jesus Christ, receive my soul, my heavenly Father; although my body is to be laid down, yet I certainly know that I shall forever remain with Thee, neither can I by any be pulled out of Thy hands."

The grace of God's Spirit oftentimes appears most, in the glory of it, when death approaches, because grace and glory are then about to meet. The soul that has followed God fully here, when it comes to depart out of the body only changes the place, not the company. This was the speech of a late reverend, holy divine of ours a little before his death: "I shall change my place, but not my company," meaning that as he had conversed with God and followed after the Lord here in this world, he was now going to converse with Him and follow after Him more fully in a better world. Death to such a soul is but God's calling it from the lower gallery of this world to the upper gallery of heaven to walk with Him there. Here the converse that Jesus Christ has with the souls of His people is compared to the converse that friends have one with another when they walk together in their galleries. Song of Solomon 7:5: "The king is held in the galleries." He not only walks with his beloved there, but is, as it were, bound. He is kept there by the bonds of love; and when death comes, then the soul is called up to the upper room, to heaven, there to follow the Lamb wherever He goes.

We read of a notable speech that Hilarion had when he was to die: "Go out, go out, my soul, why dost thou fear, why dost thou doubt? Almost these seventy years hast thou served Christ, and dost thou now fear death?" And if the end of our way at death has so much good in it, how much good will there be in the end of our way that we shall enjoy when we come to heaven!

As the consideration of the full reward in heaven was made use of before as an encouragement to those who fully follow the Lord, so now we make use of it as a strong motive to draw up our hearts to fully follow Him. It was Paul's motive to the Corinthians (1 Corinthians 15:58), persuading them to "be steadfast, unmovable, always abounding in the work of the Lord; forasmuch as ye know that your labor was not in vain in the Lord." We do not follow after shadows and fancies in following the Lord, but we seek for glory, honor, and immortality. We follow after an incorruptible crown, a glorious kingdom, an eternal inheritance, the glory of heaven. The treasures of the riches of God Himself are set before us to draw up our hearts fully to Him. It was an argument that Paul used to work upon his own spirit with. Philippians 3:14: "I press toward the mark for the prize of the high calling of God in Christ Jesus."

How full is the work of many men's spirits in their seeking after some poor, little, scant good in this world? Whereas if they had all the world, they would have only an empty husk in comparison to the glory that is set before us. They pant after the very dust. What cause is there, then, that our hearts should pant in their strong workings after those high and glorious things that are reserved in heaven for us? It was the goodness of the land of Canaan that was a strong motive to draw Caleb and Joshua's hearts fully after the Lord through many difficulties. Canaan was but a dark type of the glory of heaven that God has promised to reward His full followers with.

It was once a speech of Anselm: "If a man should serve God zealously here a thousand years, yet he would not thereby deservedly merit to be one half- day in heaven." Let us be as forward, let our hearts be as strong and zealous in God's ways as possibly they can be; yet I may say, as Abigail did to David in that particular case, "It shall repent my lord when he comes into his kingdom." So you shall never regret anything that ever you have done for the Lord when you come into your kingdom. But if it were possible there could be sorrow in heaven, you would be sorry that you did no more.

It was a speech of Gordius, a martyr, that the threats of his enemies were but as seeds from which he would reap immortality and eternal joys. So all the hardship and troubles that we meet with in our way here in following the Lord are foretastes of the glory that is to be revealed. Why, then, should anything hinder or stop us in our way?

And thus I pass to the second thing propounded in this use,

namely, to show what are the causes that hinder men from following the Lord fully, and they are five especially, which I shall but name:

1. Low apprehensions that men have of God. They do not see God in His glory, in His greatness. Surely they know not God, and therefore their hearts work so poorly after Him. Jeremiah 9:3: "They are not valiant for the truth upon the earth." And what is the reason? "For they know not me, saith the Lord." As if He should say, "Did they know Me, certainly they would be valiant for My truth."

"They that know Thy name," said the Psalmist, "will put their trust in Thee." So they that know God's name will love Him, will fear Him, will be zealous for and will follow fully after Him. The knowledge of all truths concerning heaven and hell, or any other thing that can be known, can never raise, can never enlarge the hearts of men so after the Lord as the knowledge of God Himself. And therefore, where God is little known, no marvel He is so little followed.

2. Unsound beginnings in the profession of religion are a second cause why people do not fully follow after the Lord. Their hearts are not thoroughly broken nor deeply humbled. The truths of God are not deeply rooted at first, their souls are not well principled, the foundation is not well laid. If men are not well principled at first in their entrance into the ways of God, they are likely to prove to be but shufflers and bunglers in religion all their days. If cloth is not wrought well at first, though it shows fair in the loom yet it will shrink when it gets wet. The cause why many so shrink when they get wet, when they come to suffer anything in the ways of religion, is that their hearts were not well wrought at first.

3. A third cause is the strength of engagements. Their hearts

are so wrapped in them, so glued to them, that it is exceedingly painful to get them loosed. They are so near and dear to a corrupt heart. It is said of Esau that he looked on the pottage and it was so red. So they look upon their engagements, and are fully content. It is so grievious to be taken off from them that they rather suffer their hearts to be taken off from God Himself. When engagements have taken possession of the heart, then how hard is it to work anything upon the judgments of men! It is hard to get the mind to view the truths of God, to get it to search into them, to consider them. It is ready to close with the least objection against them, to catch hold of the least advantage to cast them off; and if truths are so clear that a man cannot but see them, as conscience for the present is overpowered with them, yet if the heart is not taken off from engagements, it will fetch about again to see if something may not be gotten against those truths, to break the strength of them.

But where the heart is taken off from engagements, how easily do the truths prevail! How soon is the heart brought fully to close with them! 2 Samuel 22:33: "God," said David, "maketh my way perfect." The word is: "He frees my way." So it is translated by some, "He frees it from snares." And this is a great mercy. Hence Psalm 18:32, where this thanksgiving of David's is again repeated. There the word is translated: "He hath given my way to be perfect." This is a good gift indeed, for God to make a man's ways free and clear before Him, to take off the temptations that engaged and ensnared his spirit. And then, see 2 Samuel 22:34: "He maketh my feet as hinds' feet." Oh, how swiftly and powerfully then may the soul run in God's ways when it is thus freed! Psalm 119:44–45: "I shall keep Thy law continually, forever and ever, and I will walk at liberty." When the heart is at liberty, then it goes on continually, forever and ever, in following the Lord. But if there is any secret engagement in it, it will be weary, and at one time or another will leave off. A man who is fettered can neither go quickly nor continue long.

4. A fourth thing that hinders men in following God fully is going out in the strength of their own resolutions, not in any strength that they receive out of the fullness of Jesus Christ. They trust their own promises more than God's. Luther reports that Staupitz, a German divine, acknowledged that before he came to understand aright the free and powerful grace of Jesus Christ he vowed and resolved a hundred times against some particular sin, and never could get power over it. At last he saw the reason to be that he was trusting his own resolutions.

5. A fifth cause is meeting with more difficulties in God's ways than we made account of. Christians think only of the good and sweet things they shall meet with in God's ways, but cast not in their thoughts what the troubles are likely to be that they shall find in them. Joseph dreamed of the preferment and honor that he would have above his brethren, but dreamed not of being sold into Egypt, nor of his imprisonment there. Christians should, at the first entrance into God's ways, expect the utmost difficulties. They should enter upon those terms, ready to encounter great troubles, if they mean to follow God fully in them. It is a shame for any Christian to account any trouble that he meets with in God's ways to be as a strange thing unto him. Because the Lord had taken Paul as a chosen vessel unto Himself, and purposed to draw his heart fully after Him, observe how God dealt with him in his first entrance into His way. Acts 9:16: "I will show him how great things he must suffer for My name's sake."

But what, then, will take off the heart and carry it fully after the Lord? These three things will do it:

First, the real sight and thorough sense of sin as the greatest evil. When God leads His people weeping and with supplications, then He brings them into a straight way wherein they shall not stumble. In Jeremiah 31:9, and again in Jeremiah 50:4, the Lord said that His people shall "go weeping, and seek the Lord their God; they shall ask the way to Zion, with their faces thitherward, saying, 'Come, let us join ourselves to the Lord in a perpetual covenant that shall not be forgotten.' " When they are led weeping in a thorough sense of their sin, *then* their faces are set toward Zion, and *then* they are willing to join themselves to God in a perpetual covenant.

The second thing that will take off the heart fully is the clear sight of God in these two considerations:

In relation to ourselves, to see how there is all good in Him for us to enjoy fully, though we have nothing but Him alone. Whatever we would have in any creature, in any way so far as is good for us, it is to be had in Him. When the soul is thoroughly convinced of this, it comes off sweetly and flows fully after the Lord.

And also, consider God in relation to all other good, that nothing else has any true goodness in it but in reference and subordination to Him.

The third thing that will take off the heart fully is the fear of God and the fear of eternity powerfully falling upon the soul, deeply making an impression on it. For the fear of God, take 2 Corinthians 7:1: "Perfect your holiness in the fear of God." The fear of God is a great means to bring your holiness to perfection. See also Philippians 2:12: "Work out your salvation with fear and trembling." The fear of the eternal salvation of the soul, of the infinite consequence of it, will cause us to labor to work it out.

# Chapter Six

# It Is the Choiceness of a Man's Spirit that Causes Him to Follow God Fully

From the reference that this following God fully has to the excellency of Caleb's spirit, the doctrine that arises is this: it is the choiceness and excellency of a man's spirit that causes him to follow God fully.

Comets that are called blazing stars soon vanish because of the baseness of the matter out of which they are, but stars in the firmament continue because they are of a heavenly substance. So there are many blazing professors of religion who rise high for a while, but at last they come to nothing because their spirits are base and vile. But those who have heavenly and choice spirits go on in their way, and finish their course to the honor of God and His truth. Proverbs 11:5: "The righteousness of the perfect shall direct his way; but the wicked shall fall." Ezekiel 36:26–27: "A new heart will I give you, and a new spirit will I put within you . . . And cause you to walk in My statutes, and ye shall keep My judgments, and do them." This new spirit will cause a man to walk in God's statutes. A man of such a spirit shall certainly keep his judgments and do them even to the end.

It is not strength of parts that will carry a man through, nor strength of argument, nor strength of conviction, nor strength of natural conscience, nor strength of resolution, nor strength of common grace. It is only the choice, excellent spirit, that other spirit of which we have spoken so much before.

In this point I shall follow these three things:

Show what there is in this spirit that carries on a man fully.

Show why only this can do it.

Apply it.

First, it is the choiceness of a man's spirit that causes him to go fully after God, for:

1. By this a man comes to have a more full presence of God with him than any other man can have. Such a man is nearer unto God than others. He has more of the nature of God than others. He is more capable of the presence of God than others. And God delights to let out Himself more to him than to others. These "are filled with all the fullness of God," according to the expression of the apostle in Ephesians 3:19. Now this fullness of God in their spirits must carry them on because it so satisfies them that they feel no need of other things. Empty spirits are always sucking and drawing comfort from the creatures that are about them, and hence it is that their hearts are taken off from God so much. Again, a spirit that is filled with God is not so sensible of any evils that are without as empty spirits are. When the body is filled with good nourishment, with good blood and spirits, it is not as sensible of cold and alteration of weather as the body that is empty and filled only with wind.

2. The choiceness of a man's spirit raises it to converse with high things, and so carries it above the rubs, snares, and hindrances that are below. And being above these, it goes on freely

and fully in its course, and is not in the danger of miscarrying as other poor spirits are who converse so much with the things upon the earth. Birds that fly high are not caught by the fowler; they are not taken by his net or pitfall, as others are who are upon the ground. Proverbs 15:24: "The way of life is above to the wise, that he may depart from hell beneath." It is the act of keeping his way above that delivers him from the dangers and snares that are laid for him below. Thunders and lightnings, tempests and storms make no alteration in the highest region. So the threats and oppositions against the ways of godliness, and all the troubles that the world causes, make no alterations in heavenly hearts that keep above. When the tree grows low, it is subject to be bitten by the beasts; but when it is grown up on high it is out of danger. The lower the heart is, the nearer to the earth, the more danger; but when it is gotten up on high, the danger is passed. And now what should hinder it from its full growing up to its full measure in Christ?

3. The choiceness of a man's spirit changes his end, and so carries him on fully after the Lord. For when the end is changed, all is changed; when there are but particular changes, it is a certain argument that the highest end is not changed. But when that is changed, there must of necessity be a universal change upon these two grounds:

First, because the last end is always loved for itself, and therefore it is infinitely loved.

Second, it is the rule of all other things that are under it; the good of all things under it is measured by it, and is subordinate to it.

4. This choiceness of spirit causes a suitableness, a sympathy between the frame of the heart and the ways of holiness. Now sympathies, first, are always between the general natures of things, and not individuals, not particulars. For example,

where there is a sympathy between one creature and another, it is always between the whole kind of those creatures. Wherever such natures are found, there will be this agreement.

We may see it more clearly in that which is contrary, in the contrariety of nature that we call antipathy. It is not between any particulars so much as between the whole natures of things. Between the wolf and the sheep there is such a contrariety. Now the nature of the wolf is not so much contrary to any particular sheep, but to the whole nature of a sheep, wherever the nature of it is found, and therefore to all sheep.

Thus it is in the soul: where there is such a kind of opposition of it against sin, it is not against any particular sin so much as against the whole nature of sin, wherever it is. So where there is such an agreement that we call a sympathy, it is not so much with any particular way of holiness or particular act, but with the whole nature of holiness wherever it is found. And therefore such a soul must follow God fully.

Again, sympathies always work without labor and pain, and therefore where there is such an agreement between the frame of the heart and the ways of God, the heart must work fully because it works delightfully.

Yet further, this agreeableness of sympathy is deeply rooted in the very principles of the creature. It is founded in its very being, and therefore it must work strongly and constantly. Vain reasonings, carnal objections, subtle arguments, and strong oppositions can never prevail against the soul, where there is this deep-rooted agreeableness between the frame of it and the ways of holiness.

But that you may see further what a wonderful agreeableness grace makes between the spirits of the godly and the law of God, which is the rule of those ways wherein God would have the soul to follow Him in, observe the several expressions by which the Scripture sets it out:

> First, it is written on the tablets of their hearts.
> Second, it is their meditation day and night (Psalm 1).
> Third, it is the joy of their souls (Psalm 119:14 and 47).
> Fourth, they love it above gold, above fine gold.
> Fifth, their hearts break for the longing they have after it.
> Sixth, they lift up their hands to it (Psalm 119:48).
> Seventh, their mouths talk of it (Psalm 119:13 and 46).
> Eighth, their feet run in it (Psalm 119:32).
> Ninth, their soul keeps it (Psalm 119:167).
> Tenth, they will never forget it (Psalm 119:16).
> Eleventh, they give up their members as instruments of the

righteousness of it (Romans 6:13).

And last, to name no more (though there are many more expressions in Scripture to set this out) they apply their hearts to it, to fulfill it always even to the end (Psalm 119:103).

5. This choiceness of spirit causes a man to look to his duty, and not to regard what may follow. The thing that hinders most persons in their following the Lord is want of this; it is not want of conviction what should be done, but the reasonings of their heart about the hard and troublesome consequences that will follow if the things are done. But a true, gracious heart says only, "Let me know what is my duty; let the right be done, though heaven and earth meet together."

6. The choiceness of a man's spirit causes a man, if he looks at any consequences that may follow upon this way, to look only at the last issue of all, what his way will prove in his last conclusion, how things will go with him when he comes to the last trial, what will be the ultimate end of all. Will it then be peace? Shall I then be glad of these ways I now walk in?

7. The choiceness of a man's spirit strengthens it against the impressions that sensitive objects are prone to leave upon soft and weak spirits. Most men have their spirits formed and fashioned according to sensitive objects. It is not what they apprehend in abstract notions that works upon them, let them be what they will; yet, when they have to deal with sensitive things, the sweetness, the desirableness, the glory of them works the most powerfully. Their hearts are altered according to the impression that they leave upon them, and this is great weakness and an effeminate softness of spirit. Hence the word translated "effeminate" in 1 Corinthians 6:9 signifies soft-spirited men.

This distemper in the spirit is like that in the flesh when it is corrupted with the dropsy. The flesh is soft, and if you put your finger to it the impression of your finger sticks in it and pits the flesh. So the impression of sensitive objects sticks in distempered, weak, soft, spirits as it was in the other spies who were sent with Caleb and Joshua. The terrible things they saw in the land stuck mightily in their hearts. They brought with them the impression of them fastened in their spirits. Hence Numbers 13:33, according to the translation of the Greek translators, is: "They brought the fear of the land with them." But this choiceness of spirit that was in Caleb, and is in those who were truly godly, keeps from this. And there must be this firmness in the spirit of a man or else it will never carry him after the Lord fully. 2 Samuel 22:26: "With the upright Thou wilt show Thyself upright." The word translated "upright" signifies strong and perfect. Strength is required, and that more than ordinary too, to carry on the soul to perfection.

Thus you see what there is in this choice spirit that carries it on fully after the Lord. Now there must of necessity be this, or else this full following of the Lord will never be; nothing else will do it:

1. Because the ways of God are supernatural, therefore

there must be something in the spirit of man that is supernatural in the spirits of godly men. We see it in the effects, and we know it is above reason and all natural principles whatsoever. But what it is is very hard to express; and therefore men of parts in the world are mad to think that any should imagine that those who are of weaker parts than themselves, should have anything in them to carry them on in other ways than they walk in; which they do not understand, because they do not know what that thing is which is called supernatural. They will rather think it a conceit and fancy than any real excellency. Because they can apprehend other things better than others, they think, why should they not apprehend this better than others, if there were any real excellency in it.

2. The ways of God are not only above nature, but contrary to nature, and therefore there must be some special choiceness of spirit to carry a man on in them. There must be a contrary stream to overpower the stream of nature; and this stream must be fed by some living fountain or else he will never hold out. In following after the Lord, all natural abilities and common grace will do no more than stop the stream of corrupt nature. They cannot so overpower it as to carry the soul another way; but the work of grace in this choiceness of spirit will do it.

3. The stream of times and examples of men are exceeding strong, and it is not a little matter that will carry on the soul against them. The dead fish is carried down the stream, though the wind serves to blow it up. All natural abilities of the soul will no more help a man against the stream of examples than the wind can carry the dead fish up the stream; but if life were put into the fish, it would be able then to move against the wind and stream too.

4. There are so many strong, alluring temptations wherein the wiles, subtleties, and depths of Satan are very powerful to

draw the heart away from God, that unless there is some special work of God's grace to give wisdom to discern the deceits of sin, to make the soul spiritually subtle, to find out the cunning devices of Satan and to discern the danger of them, the soul most certainly could never hold on in the way of following after the Lord.

5. There are so many troubles and oppositions that it meets with in this way that most certainly would drive it out were it not for some choice work of God's grace in it; but this choiceness of spirit will carry a man through all them. It is God's promise in Isaiah 59:19: "When the enemy shall come in like a flood, the Spirit of the Lord shall lift up a standard against him." We made use of this Scripture before for opposition to strong corruptions; but it is true here now for the resisting of strong spiritual enemies, of strong oppositions. When they come in like a flood against the soul to carry it out of God's ways, the Spirit of God in it lifts up a standard against them; and were it not for this, it could not hold. It is this good and sound constitution of the soul that makes it endure those oppositions that it meets with. As anguish from heat may be greater than that which arises from a good constitution, but it is not able to resist cold, so there may be a natural violence in a man's spirit for awhile in the profession of religion which may seem to be zeal, but not arising from the good constitution of the soul. When troubles come it vanishes, giving no strength at all.

6. There are so many scandals and reproaches that rise against the ways of God, so many aspersions that are cast upon them, that if a man has no more than an ordinary spirit he most certainly will be offended. "Blessed are they that are not offended in me," said Christ. It is a great blessing when scandal falls out, and when we see grievous aspersions cast upon God's ways, yet we need not to be offended. There needs to be some-

thing more than ordinary light to reveal to a man the certainty of that good there is in the ways of God. He needs to be sure of his principles, and know in whom he has believed.

7. Yea, God many times hides Himself from His servants while they are following after Him. And this oftentimes proves the sorest temptation of all, and a greater discouragement than all the rest; for as for oppositions, scandals, and reproaches, these are things they make account of, and can often lightly pass them over. But when God hides His face, this puts them at a loss: now they are in the dark and know not what to do. Christ was not much troubled at the reproaches of men, at the oppositions He met with from them, for they said, "He despised the shame, and endured the cross" (Hebrews 12:2).

But when His Father hid His face from Him, then He was in an agony; then His spirit began to be amazed; then His soul was sorrowful to death; then He fell groveling on the ground; then He sweated drops of water and blood; then He cried out, "My God, My God, why hast Thou forsaken Me?" These spiritual desertions, in their degree, God's servants often meet with in their way, so that if they had not choice spirits, some special work of God in their souls, they would certainly fall and sink in it.

Now, put all these together and we see that it is not every ordinary spirit that is likely to go on fully after the Lord. It must be something extraordinary that preserves a spark in the midst of waves, that preserves a candle light in the midst of storms and tempests.

Never wonder, then, or be offended to see so many fall off from God. Few men have choice spirits. Those who are godly expect no other from most professors, and therefore they are not troubled when they see this fall out. "They went out from us, because they were not of us," said the apostle in 1 John 2:19. Wicked men are offended because they know not what the work of grace means; and hence, if they see a man make profession of religion, they make no distinction, as though there were as much to be expected from him as from another; as though the cause of God fell when he fell. No such conclusion follows if you see men's spirits proud, slight, earthly, sensual, or carried with a greater violence than their principles will bear. I do not mean that, though their affections may not sometimes go beyond their knowledge, but by principles I mean the rooted graces of God in their hearts, as one may perceive in some. There are not graces rooted suitable to their expressions and outward ways; and when you see not an evenness in the ways of men, then never expect from them any full following of the Lord. And if they fall off, be not troubled; let it be no more than you made account of beforehand would be.

Hence the world is mistaken who judge it stoutness and stubbornness of spirit in God's servants who will go on in the ways of godliness. They are seen as a kind of inflexible people; there is no persuading them; there is no dealing with them. No, it is not stubbornness; it is the choiceness of their spirits that makes them do as they do.

You judge it stubbornness because you do not know the principles upon which they go. I confess, if I see a man stand constantly in His way who will not be moved by the persuasions of others, if I do not understand the reasons upon which he goes, I cannot but think it stoutness. And this is your case; but if you did but know what are their reasons, what are the powerful motives that draw them on in the ways of God, you would not have such thoughts of them. "Their spirits within them constrain them," as Elihu says of himself in another case (Job 32:18).

Take these convincements, that it is not stubbornness but choiceness of spirit that carries them on so immoveable in their way.

1. In other things they are as yielding, as tractable, as easy to be persuaded, as any men. It is only in the matter of the Lord their God they are thus. They can bear burdens upon their shoulders, and cry out, and resist as little as any. If you compel them to go a mile, they will be content, if they may do good, to go two; yea, as far as the shoes of the preparation of the gospel of peace will carry them. Who can bear wrongs and injuries from men better than they? Stubborn-spirited men cannot do thus.

2. Stubbornness is joined with desire for revenge, but in these dispositions there is all pity and compassion. They pray for those who oppose them. When they are reviled, they revile not again. If sometimes their corruptions should be stirred, they are ashamed and confounded in their own thoughts for what they have done. They mourn and lament in the bitterness of their spirits for it.

3. Stubborn dispositions are not contracted all of a sudden. It is by degrees and continuance of time that nature is altered; but this disposition of being unmovable in God's ways comes many times even all of a sudden, as soon as ever the heart is turned, which is an evidence that a new principle has been put into it.

4. Stubborn hearts do not usually seek God to uphold them, to strengthen them, to bless them in that way. They do not bless God for being with them, helping them to persist in their way as God's servants do. They go to God to get strength to enable them to be immovable. They give God the glory of it, when they have found themselves enabled to withstand temptations.

5. Those who are of stubborn dispositions are not usually most stubborn when their heart is most broken with afflictions. Stout hearts, in prosperity, are unyielding; there is no dealing

with them then. Their hearts are immediately up. If you move them to anything they have no mind to, their words are stout, their answers are fierce; but let afflictions come, then, as Isaiah 29:4: "Their hearts are brought down, and they speak as one out of the ground, and their speech is low, as one out of the dust." Then they are willing to hear what you say. They are like the young gallant that Solomon speaks of in Proverbs 5; there was no speaking to him in his prosperity, but when his flesh and body were consumed, then he mourned at last and cried out in Proverbs 5:12–13, "How have I hated instruction, and my heart despised reproof! I have not obeyed the voice of my teacher." But now, those who are godly, in their greatest afflictions, when their hearts are most broken, when God humbles them most, even then they are most settled and unmovable in the way they walked in before. And it is then the greatest grief of their souls that they walked no closer with God in it than they did. Have other thoughts than of God's people than you have had; do not accuse of stubbornness what you do not understand. Think to yourselves that there may be something in their spirits more than you know of.

Let those who have this excellent, choice spirit encourage themselves in that surely it will enable them to follow God fully.

Let them know, first, that though they are weak, if their spirits be right, if of the right kind, they shall certainly hold out. That which Christ said for the comfort of the church of Philadelphia in Revelation 3:8, they may apply for theirs: "Thou hast a little strength," said Christ, "and hast kept My word, and hast not denied My name." A little strength, if it is right, if it is the strength of a sound spirit, will carry on the soul to keep God's Word, and enable it not to deny His name.

Second, therefore, Christ is filled will all fullness of all grace, that out of His fullness you may receive grace for grace. That spirit by which He is so plentifully anointed is for you.

OBJECTION. "But I am afraid my spirit is not this choice spirit, and therefore I shall not hold out in following the Lord."
ANSWER. I ask you these questions. First, is it a broken, humble spirit in sense of your weakness and wants?

Second, that which you do, though but weakly, is it upon divine grounds, and have you divine ends?

Third, does the sight of your weakness make you cling and cleave unto Jesus Christ?

Fourth, when you lose God in following Him, are you sensible of the want of His presence, and do you never leave crying and seeking till you enjoy Him again?

Certainly, this is a true choice spirit that will carry on fully in following the Lord when thousands of glorious hypocrites shall vanish and come to nothing.

If this choiceness of Spirit is the only thing that will fully carry after the Lord, then let us learn to look to our spirits. "Keep thy heart with all diligence, for out of it come the issues of life" (Proverbs 4:23). Do not so much complain of temptations, oppositions, or troubles you meet with, but look to your spirits and all is well. If there is the spirit of love and a sound mind, there will be the spirit of power; for these are joined together by the Apostle. There need not be the spirit of fear, for the spirit of a sound mind and the spirit of fear are opposed one to another in the same place.

QUESTION. But wherein should we look to our spirits?
ANSWER. First, take heed to your judgments. Keep your judgments clear for God and His truth. As it is said in Isaiah 33:6, wisdom and knowledge, preserving the judgments of men right and sound, are the stability of men's hearts. Take heed your

judgments come not to be altered, to think otherwise of God's ways than you did before, to have other opinions of them. Though there may be many weaknesses, yet if the judgment is kept right, all may do well; but if the leprosy gets into the head, then the soul is in a dangerous condition. In Leviticus 13:44, when the priest looks upon the leprous man and sees the plague has gotten into his head, the text says, "He shall pronounce him utterly unclean for the plague is in his head." The priest was to pronounce none to be utterly unclean but such who had the plague in their heads.

Second, labor to keep conscience clear; take heed of pollution there; take heed of a breach in your spirit there, for that will weaken it much: conscience is the strong tower of the soul; if the truth of God gets out from there, the strength of the soul is gone.

Third, labor to keep your heart low and humble. When the flesh swells, it cannot bear any hard thing upon it. Though a member grows bigger when it swells, yet it grows weaker. So it is with the soul.

Fourth, labor to keep the spirit heavenly. Mixture of dross will weaken it. Convince your soul that a little of the creature will serve turn to carry you through your pilgrimage well enough. One told a philosopher, "If you will be content to please Dionysius, you need not feed upon green herbs." The philosopher answered him, "And if you will be content to feed upon green herbs, you need not please Dionysius." So if men would be content with a little in the world, to be in a low and mean condition, they need not flatter. Those things that draw others from following after the Lord would not move them at all.

Fifth, labor to keep yourself in a continually trembling frame, abiding in the fear of the Lord all the day long. The fear of the Lord causes men to depart from evil. Meditate upon the fear of the Lord continually.

Last, keep your spirit continually working. Many things have much power in them while they are in motion, but are weak when the motion ceases. Sin is very strong while it is in motion, but when afflictions stop the motion, the truths of God have more power over it. So while grace is acting it is strong, but if it grows dull it grows weak and is soon turned aside. Thus we, looking to our spirits, shall be able to follow the Lord fully and finish our course in peace.

*Finis*